Praise for

BECOMING WILD: HOW ANIMAL CULTURES RAISE FAMILIES, CREATE BEAUTY, AND ACHIEVE PEACE

NAMED A BEST BOOK OF THE YEAR BY
THE NEW YORK TIMES AND *KIRKUS REVIEWS*

"Fascinating ... [*Becoming Wild*] gives the reader a sense of being near these creatures and experiencing some of the most seductive environments on Earth ... Safina's prose achieves the elusive goal of being both informative and luminously evocative."
—*The Wall Street Journal*

"Combining the knowledge of a seasoned scientist with the skills of a good storyteller, Safina invites us to leave our cultural worlds and enter animals' ones ... *Becoming Wild* deserves to be remembered."
—NPR

"[Safina] turns the human view of animal cultures on its head ... *Becoming Wild* demands that we wake up and realize that we are intrinsically linked to our other-than-human neighbors."
—*The Telegraph* (UK)

"[Safina] shows us something too often overlooked in research and in conservation: who animals are, and how they live ... [And] it's the stories of Safina's days with these animals that move us."
—*The New York Times*

ALSO BY CARL SAFINA

Beyond Words: What Wolves and Dogs Think and Feel
(A Young Reader's Adaptation)

*Beyond Words: What Elephants and Whales Think and
Feel* (A Young Reader's Adaptation)

Nina Delmar: The Great Whale Rescue

LEARNING TO BE WILD

HOW ANIMALS ACHIEVE PEACE, CREATE BEAUTY, AND RAISE FAMILIES

CARL SAFINA

ROARING BROOK PRESS
New York

Published by Roaring Brook Press
Roaring Brook Press is a division of Holtzbrinck Publishing Holdings Limited
Partnership
120 Broadway, New York, NY 10271 • mackids.com

Our books may be purchased in bulk for promotional, educational,
or business use. Please contact your local bookseller or the Macmillan Corporate
and Premium Sales Department at (800) 221-7945 ext. 5442 or by email at
MacmillanSpecialMarkets@macmillan.com.

Library of Congress Cataloging-in-Publication Data is available.

First edition, 2023
Book design by Aurora Parlagreco
Printed in the United States of America by Lakeside Book Company,
Harrisonburg, Virginia

ISBN 978-1-250-83825-4 (hardcover)
1 3 5 7 9 10 8 6 4 2

This book is dedicated to you, *because your interest has already brought you closer to the animals. You'll get even closer in the pages that follow.*

The more the habits of any particular animal are studied by a naturalist, the more he attributes to reason and the less to unlearnt instincts.
—Charles Darwin, *The Descent of Man*, 1871

CONTENTS

From Left: *Hawa, Musa, Simon*

PROLOGUE

A LITTLE CHIMPANZEE RIDES ON his mother's back to a waterhole. It's the dry season, so only scattered shallow puddles remain. It's hot. Everyone has been in a distant fruit tree all morning and after trekking through thick forest, the whole group is keen with thirst. The mother searches out some moss, wads it into a kind of sponge, dips it into a tiny puddle, puts the wet sponge into her mouth, and presses out a drink. Her little prince hops off, taps her until she gives him the sponge, and does the same. After this crucial lesson about how to quench thirst in the dry season, he and his mother relax enough to find his friends and indulge in socializing.

A flock of scarlet macaws comes out of deep rainforest like flaming comets—several dozen big, bright birds with streaming tails and hot colors. With much self-generated fanfare they settle into high trees above a steep riverbank. They're noisy and playful. If this is the serious business of their lives, they seem to be enjoying themselves and each other. Even within the flock it's easy to see that many travel as close-together pairs. Following one such pair is a third bird, a hefty juvenile from last year's breeding season, continually begging and bothering their parents. The other year-old macaws have learned a more dignified independence—if you'd call hanging upside down, fooling around, and flirting "dignified"—and have begun sorting themselves into their own young social lives.

Meanwhile, in tropical water two miles deep, a defenseless infant sperm whale waits at the warm, sunlit surface while her mother hunts squid in night-black frigid water thousands of feet below. Like a balloon on a string the baby follows her unseen mother. She is hearing the clicks of Mom's sonar. Nearby, the baby's aunt stands guard and waits her turn to dive and hunt. At the first signal of a threat to the baby, the whole family comes rushing up from far beneath the indigo sea.

The stories in this book are about animal cultures. The natural does not always come naturally. Many animals must learn from their elders how to be who they were born to be. They must learn the local quirks, how to make a living, and how to communicate and be heard effectively in a particular place among their particular group. Cultural learning spreads skills (such as the knowledge of what is food and how to get it), creates identity and a sense of belonging within a group (rather than with other groups), and carries on traditions (such as effective courtship practices).

For many species, culture is both crucial and fragile. Long before a population declines to numbers low enough to *seem* threatened with extinction, their special cultural knowledge, earned and passed down over long generations, can begin disappearing.

We become who we are not by genes alone. Culture is also a form of inheritance. Culture stores important information not in gene pools, but in minds. Pools of knowledge—tools, skills, preferences, songs, and dialects—get relayed through generations like a torch. Culture is: ways of doing things that are learned from others. And culture itself changes and evolves, often bestowing adaptability more flexibly and rapidly than genetic evolution could. An individual receives genes only from their parents, but can receive culture from anyone and everyone in their social group. You're not born with culture; you have to learn it.

For the last thirty years or so the diversity of all living things, "biodiversity," has been thought of as operating at three main levels: the genetic diversity within each species, the diversity among species, and the diversity of habitats (grasslands, forests, deserts, oceans, and so on). But there is a fourth level in living diversity, and it is just now becoming recognized: cultural diversity. Culture is knowledge and skills that travel from individual to individual and generation to generation. It is learned *socially*. Individuals pick it up from other individuals. It is knowledge that doesn't come from instinct alone. It's not inherited in genes. What is learned and shared is culture.

What is cultural becomes obvious if not everyone does it. Everyone eats; eating isn't culture. Not everyone eats with chopsticks; chopsticks are part of culture. All chimpanzees climb trees; that's not cultural. Some chimpanzee populations—not all—crack nuts with hammer stones and anvils. That's cultural.

Group-to-group differences in customs, traditions, practices, and tools show what is cultural. These things apply to us humans— and to quite a few other cultural animals.

It's highly practical for members of a species to rely on social learning. If someone in your community has already figured out what's safe and what to avoid, sometimes it pays to "do the done thing." If you go it alone, you might learn the hard way what is poisonous, or where it's dangerous to go.

Social learning goes on all around us. But it's subtle; you have to look carefully and for a long time. This book is one deep, clear look into things that are difficult to see.

We will see how, if you're the chimpanzee Musa, or the macaw Tabasco, or the sperm whale Pinchy, you, too, experience your wild life with the understanding that you are an individual in a particular community that does things in certain ways. We'll see that cultures provide answers to the question of how to live where one lives. That's very true for us, too.

Learning "how we live" from others is human. But learning from others is also raven. Ape and whale. Parrot. Even honey-bee. Many creatures must *learn* almost everything about how to become who they will be.

The chimps, parrots, and whales we will visit represent three major themes of culture: social living creates tensions that cul-ture must soothe, social living creates identity and family, and the enormous implications of beauty. These species and many others in these pages will be our teachers. We will learn something from each that will widen our appreciation of being alive in the world.

By going deep into nature and looking at individual crea-tures in their free-living communities, we are going to get a very privileged glimpse behind the curtain of life on Earth. Watching as knowledge, skills, and customs flow among other species provides us with a new understanding of what is constantly going on unseen, beyond humanity. It will help inform the answer to that most urgent of questions: Who are our traveling companions in the journey of this planet? Who are we here with?

That's our present expedition. Ready?

Baby chimpanzees love to play. They are fantastic climbers.
Mom is always watching closely, making sure they are okay.

REALM ONE: ACHIEVING PEACE

CHIMPANZEES
Budongo Forest of Uganda

PEACE

ONE

BEFORE I CAN SHOULDER MY pack, Cat and Kizza vanish into the undergrowth as though swallowed into a green portal. I dart in and scurry toward the sounds ahead. Now and then I glimpse Cat, glancing over her shoulder to make sure she hasn't lost me.

I catch up and she whispers, "It's Alf. Alf can disappear."

Alf is disappearing now; we must hurry.

He'd just eased his dark, human-like figure down a thick vine, planted his feet on the ground, lowered himself to the knuckles of his hands, then straight and purposefully walked off into thick vegetation. Now he's moving at a challenging pace.

Alf's all-fours gait is well suited to these thickets. Upright, on two tippy legs, we're slowed by head-high leafy branches and ankle-tangling vines.

Cat and Kizza glide through the thick greenery. I'm new here. And if I lose my companions, I'll be completely lost on my first day in this African forest. Coming back to find me would disrupt their research for the morning. They can't afford that loss of time. I can't afford that kind of a start to my visit. I struggle to keep them in sight.

After a few minutes Alf slows, and as I catch up I get a good view of him. By following Alf, we're studying how chimpanzees manage their day and their social agenda. Cat Hobaiter's life's work is to learn how chimpanzees here in the Budongo Forest of Uganda use gestures—often very subtle ones—to communicate. Expertly aided by research assistant Kizza Vincent, Cat looks deep into chimpanzee life.

Cat Hobaiter

Alf

Alf joins several other chimpanzees. One, backlit high up in a tree, has a clinging baby. I raise my binoculars. Kizza whispers, "Dat is Shy."

"How," I ask, "can you tell who that is?"

Kizza replies in light zephyrs of speech. "If I see your shape, you walking away, I know it is you."

It's that easy?

Cat affirms. She just glances—face, build, stride—recognition is instant.

The chimpanzees certainly differ. Some have a boxy body build, some lanky. Their complexions range: pale, brown, mottled, freckled, coal black. Faces that are flatter or rounder, have heavier or finer features, differ in shapes and wrinkle patterns and higher or lower hairlines. Ears, mouths, the shapes and shades of lips— all vary. Hair varies, butch to plush.

Here in their easy mix of pale and dark faces, chimpanzees have a solution to humanity's fundamental obsession with skin differences. Chimps suffer none of that awful thing; we alone saddle ourselves with those manufactured hatreds. But as I'll learn, they have their own self-inflicted issues. I'll also learn: a preference for peace, within a penchant for war, is another thing we have in common.

Masariki, an adolescent male with distinctive oval eyes and a flat face, rests with his usual companion, Gerald. When Masariki was young, Gerald would help him across gaps in the trees by bending branches or by using his own body as a bridge. Masariki was an orphan. He and Gerald might be siblings, but Gerald is dark-faced and Masariki a lighter shade of pale. Gerald probably adopted him.

Kizza Vincent

Fifteen-year-old Daudi appears with twenty-year-old Macallan, who is missing his left thumb. Cat brings us startlingly close.

I wonder out loud why they are not apprehensive of me.

"Actually," Cat informs me, "they've been watching you. But they don't fear people who are with me and Kizza."

Cat Hobaiter has been working here in Budongo Forest for a decade and a half. Athletic, late thirties, sporting a dark bob of hair, she is among other things a very strong walker. A child refugee from war in Lebanon, Cat eventually earned a doctoral diploma from the University of St. Andrews in Scotland, where she is now a professor. When she first came here, she found chimpanzees "addictive," she says.

Chimpanzees seem very familiar to most people, of course. And as with most "very familiar" things, if we stop to think for a moment we realize we actually know almost nothing about them. We know they are cute as babies. We may think of Jane Goodall lovingly cradling an adorable young chimp (yet not wonder what happened to the mother). We may know that they normally live in Africa. And not much else.

About seven million years ago our common ancestor started to split into new species, and *Pan* (chimpanzee and bonobo) and *Homo* (human) began separate trajectories. (The gorilla had begun its journey much earlier, about ten million years ago. The orangutan, roughly fifteen.) Various *Homo* species—possibly up to twenty species of humans—evolved and flourished. They include the widespread *Homo heidelbergensis*, Asia's "Denisovans," the Naledi in South Africa, and many others. *Homo erectus* first mastered fire making. Neanderthal bones with healed breaks and evident disabilities indicate their care for the disabled. Some disappeared; some became us. Our species is the closest *living* relative of the chimpanzee and bonobo. Together with gorillas, chimpanzees, bonobos, and orangutans, humans are in a group called Hominidae or "the great apes."

Compared to chimpanzees' brains, humans' brains have no new parts, and run using the same neurotransmitters. Human and chimpanzee DNA is 98 to 99 percent similar. Chimpanzees and bonobos share more than 99 percent of their DNA. We are so closely related genetically because we share a common ancestor species. A few million years ago—a long time for us; but very recently in the long, long history of life on Earth—one ape-like species slowly split into several. One of *those* lines became chimpanzees. Another eventually became our human species. The differences that make humans human, chimps chimp, and bonobos bonobo are small. This closeness and this family history are indicated by our similar body plans and our mostly identical genes.

The social world of a chimpanzee is a complex web of friends, relatives, and ambitions.

Cat explains. "It's not just a matter of who you like. It's also, who are your allies? Who is low risk for you and for your children? Who knows the food trees?"

Chimpanzees often move in groups. You can be with whomever you please. Certain individuals spend part of every day together; some spend part of each day alone.

There *are* some rules: One, mothers and young children are inseparable. Two, though parties are fluid within a community, which *community* you belong to is rigid. Third, male rank matters—a lot.

The basic social unit of chimpanzee life is the "community." A community holds and defends territory—sometimes violently—against other communities.

As with us, group stability depends on a mental *concept* of "we." Crucially, young chimps watch Mom's social interactions, learning how to act, who they'll be with, where to go when, and situations to avoid.

Male chimpanzees remain in the community of their birth for all their lives. Males anchor a community to its land, its customs, and its identity through generations, over centuries. Most females move at adolescence, permanently, into a nearby community. This often means moving in with chimps who have been her birth community's territorial enemies. It's a fraught transition. Upon arrival in her new community, where she will likely live for the rest of her life, she might be welcomed, attacked, or bullied by senior females.

Basically, chimpanzees live in tribal groups on tribal lands. Human-like, not human; contemporaries, not ancestors. We share deep history.

Budongo Forest, elevation three thousand feet, is an island of green surrounded by smoky haze. The rising sea of human settlement comes right to its boundary, as though the forest is the drowning shore of a shrinking continent. Budongo occupies about 460 square kilometers, twenty-five miles across the long way. Not much. Though Budongo Forest Reserve is one of the largest forests remaining in Uganda, it was heavily logged for mahogany and other woods, with much of it exported. No elephants remain here, no leopards. People may come and gather medicinal plants and firewood. People may not cut trees, or set snares for bush pigs and the small forest antelope called duikers (rhymes with "hikers"). But people do.

The researchers here have named several chimpanzee communities after parts of the forest. This community that's the focus of Cat's research is Waibira. Adjacent to Waibira is another well-observed community called Sonso. Sonso, the smallest chimpanzee territory known anywhere, is only about eight square kilometers (three square miles). Waibira, at twice that, is still significantly smaller than average. Elsewhere, most chimp communities occupy territories of around twenty to twenty-five square kilometers. Food in Budongo is a concern. Over twenty years, the amount of fruit has declined by an estimated 10 percent, seemingly due to climate warming.

Waibira is made up of about 130 members and an unusually high proportion of adult males. Sonso has about 65 individuals. Sonso also borders the forest's edge and farmers' fields, creating problems. When Cat first arrived here the forest was different. Chimpanzees relied on different kinds of trees at different times of the year. But certain trees that are so valued by chimpanzees are also worth money, and they have been drastically depleted.

Our research station is a cluster of ground-level dormitories on the site of the former sawmill that dismantled much of the original forest. Varied wildlife is accustomed to the camp and its humans, lending a Garden of Eden air. It's normal to open your door and have two monkeys streak past your toes. Baboons of olive hue, blue monkeys with nervous eyebrows, red-tailed guenon monkeys whose striking facial markings look painted on, and velvety colobus monkeys with elegant white capes—all visit daily. Local women bend over wood fires to cook our supper of rice or cassava with beans or peas. We drink rainwater purified through porcelain filters. There is no plumbing.

The chimps fear villagers in their forest—with good reason—but have become accustomed to researchers. Cat invested years to simply get Waibira chimps to ignore her presence so she could observe them behaving naturally. Researchers provide no food. We're just here, and the chimps are used to that.

Eight or nine other chimpanzee communities here in Budongo Forest remain untamed, unnamed. Their identity, deep and absolute, is known only by them.

To truly comprehend any creature—including people—you must watch them live on their own terms. Budongo chimpanzees are in charge of their movements and decisions. Their lives are complex. Budongo's free-living chimpanzees are homeschooled in their own traditions, with the knowledge of mothers conveyed to children through ages of deep, wild history.

PEACE

TWO

BEN, THE MOTTLE-FACED EMPEROR OF Waibira, arrives
flinging things and dragging dead branches noisily through dry
leaves. He—especially in his own opinion—must be noticed.
As "alpha," Ben has held "office" since last year. In only his late
twenties, Ben was unusually young when he attempted to take
top spot. "I wasn't expecting him to succeed," Cat offers. "But he
made it, early."

How does chimpanzee culture hold their community together
despite the intense ambitions of power-seeking males? You'd think
members might simply walk away from the threats and potential
violence. Their high-strung lifestyle includes the continual drama
of males plotting with strategic allies to either overthrow the
current dominant male and seize rank or—if you are the most
dominant male or in his circle of closest allies—to maintain dominance. Socially it can be like a pressure cooker waiting to explode.
Why don't the pressure, drama, and occasional violence make the
system fall apart? Why don't females, low-ranking males, and

more peaceful individuals just leave? Something keeps them together. Like humans in less-than-ideal social conditions, there must be some advantage to staying in the group. I'd especially like to understand chimpanzees' cultural mechanisms for reducing conflict and tensions, and for maintaining the peace—most of the time. Ben is shaking saplings, hooting, and thump-kicking the fin-like buttress roots that support the trunks of big trees like ribbony walls. The high-ranking are seldom secure. They assert and reassert with bluster and noise, because strength is mainly what they've got. But there's a lot of competing strength among chimpanzees. And willingness to use it. And ambition. So in addition, there's strategy.

Ben

"Males who rely only on strength," Cat explains, "who make a habit of attacking over minor things or taking fights further than necessary—they don't get far or don't last long. Most use a balance; a few are amazing strategists." You can play the game in different ways, Cat explains. For instance, Zefa remained second in dominance through two alphas. "You can remain in the number-two spot and get the benefits, while avoiding a lot of the stress of grabbing and holding on to the top slot. It's worked for him."

Ben's rank requires all others to acknowledge his superiority with a specific greeting called a "pant-grunt." It's required when a high-ranker must be greeted with a respectful "Hello, sir."

But today Alf doesn't pant-grunt to Ben. More surprising—he gets away with it.

"Ben's not getting due respect," Cat says. We wonder what's up.

Hierarchy is *the* preoccupation of male chimpanzee life. For them as for us, status seeking is an impulse, dominance its own reward.

Masariki

Rising up the male rank order entails calculated risk. "There's always a lot of subtle politics," Cat explains. "Who is seen with whom, who sits where, who gets up and follows. It's like who gets to go to lunch with whom." These little things clue you to building tensions well before sudden violence brings a power shift.

A possible reason for Ben's reluctance to assert his rank to Alf: Ben must be unwell. There's been a serious coughing cold going around. Almost every chimp's been sick; a couple have disappeared. Maybe today no one's up for a challenge.

From deep brush comes a chimp with a black face and a torn ear. This is Lotty, one of the regulars. In her early thirties, Lotty has a six-year old daughter. Lotty dutifully pant-grunts her acknowledgement of Ben's supreme rank, then begins grooming him.

Lotty

Lotty and Ben seem absorbed. Until—They stop. Listen attentively. Are we hearing friends or an adjacent community? They're monitoring who is where, what they're up to, what they might be up against. They always want to know: What's going on in the community?

They move. We follow. They travel on the soles of their feet like us, and on the knuckles of their hands, unlike us. They're moving off-trail, necessitating bushwhacking by us uprights. We walk single file, me last, following Cat.

A towering tree bursts above its neighbors, spreading its canopy over them. High in chimpanzee heaven, dark shapes are reaching black arms across the baby-blue dawn sky.

Alf climbs as easily as we ascend stairs, basically walking straight up the trunk. When climbing, their thumb-like big toes give them effectively four hands. Their short, thick legs propel them straight up trunks. Long arms make a ballet of it all. Shy begins her own ascent, and with a baby clinging to her belly her strength is even more impressive.

Shy stops climbing and extends an arm, her gesture of intent to her baby to use Mom's arm as a ramp onto the main trunk. Very small baby chimps are startlingly nimble and confident. He grasps a tiny vine and pulls it, holding its tip in his mouth while getting his grip on a more substantial portion, clearly understanding exactly what's needed for safety. Hanging by one arm, he swings on the vine, building momentum before making his next reach to the branch he's targeting. This little six-month-old fluffball is a crazy climber, swinging hand-over-hand through the tree with feet dangling. He's loving it. His mother watches carefully but seems confident in her child.

The chimps share this tree with half a dozen monkeys and eight huge birds with gigantic bills, white-casqued hornbills, who caw through the canopy on big, swooshy wings. This rooted, towering being grows not only figs; it grows these animals and sets them in motion among its branches. They shriek, whistle, hoot. If you think trees do not talk, you are partly right. The trees let the creatures that they grow do the talking.

The chimps' climbing and swinging, their reaching, picking, and eating, would seem absolutely to require four-limbed proficiency. But I'm noticing that the chimps now aloft include several whose hands or limbs seem impaired. Cat says that about three of every four adult chimpanzees here bears a snare's disfigurement. For many, just a scar or stiff hand. Others lack fingers or toes. Or worse. Thirty-year-old Jinja lacks her right hand; ten-year-old Andrua lacks his left; Philipo is missing a foot.

Villagers set snares for wild pigs and forest antelopes, which they eat. But the snares can catch anything. When a snare's noose closes around a chimpanzee's hand or foot, they immediately pull with all their immense strength. This force sinks the cable (bicycle brake cables are commonly used) though the skin. The panicked chimpanzee screams and spins around and around trying to free themselves. Eventually the cable twists to the breaking point, releasing the now-maimed chimp whose troubles have just begun. Some die of infection inside a week. Some survive.

"It's heartbreaking," Cat says, "to see them using their communication gestures with hands that are missing fingers." You'd think a missing hand or foot is a death sentence. But then you see one with such an impairment, see that they climb and survive despite their handicaps, sometimes with a baby on their back, getting on with life. Cat comments, "Humans at our worst; them at their best."

Up in the sunshine, Alf eats for half an hour.

Chimpanzees know and keep track of dozens of food trees and their stage of ripeness. Chimps don't *wander* in search of food. They commute. They head to trees they have in mind. If they check a tree and the fruit is far from being ripe, they'll adjust the timing of their next visit depending on whether the subsequent weeks are sunny or rainy, weather that speeds or slows ripening. "It's insane," Cat admits. "I couldn't keep track of all their trees. I couldn't do it."

Alf takes a break, lying on a broad limb between two heavy clumps of figs. Life is good for him at the moment. On the forest floor we rest against trees, watching chimps and listening to forest doves sending rhythmic coos to one another.

When Alf moves off across the forest floor, we again struggle to keep pace through vegetation so heavy it's like being in green seawater.

Suddenly we nearly stumble upon Alf, resting, half-hidden by dense foliage. He has met up with four resting chimps. But when a round of sudden *wah*s and hoots ignites them, we realize that more than a dozen chimpanzees sit hidden close in leafy shadows.

Alf utters a "resting *hoo*." He makes several long arm scratches to invite Gerald to a grooming session.

Alf sits with one arm out, a gesture suggesting that this would be the ideal spot to start grooming. Gerald understands. Gerald jabs four fingertips into Alf's hair and lifts to expose and skillfully remove dirt and any bugs. The jab-and-lift is true Budongo style, a cultural quirk here that is unlike the long raking motions chimps elsewhere use when grooming. After a minute Gerald gives Alf's head a gentle nudge with his hand, like a hair stylist might. "Move your head so I can get to your neck." For twenty minutes they indulge.

Grooming's superficial effect is parasite removal. But the much deeper function is promoting trust and alliances. The power of touch.

Humans have retained some social grooming: combing and brushing another's hair, spreading sunblock. It helps deepen or maintain the relationship. You don't have a relationship until you invest time in it, and "if you're a chimpanzee," Cat emphasizes, "you invest time by grooming."

When we say metaphorically that a man is "being groomed" for a higher rank, we're intuiting that grooming can be about male power. With chimpanzees—it is. An alpha male gets groomed most. Grooming among male chimpanzees is about establishing and maintaining social bonds needed for later cooperation in territorial defense, hunting, and taking and keeping rank.

In chimps these concerns are male things. In humans they're often male things. But in some other animals—macaque monkeys for example—females do more grooming than males. In bonobo society, power is female, and female bonobos use their power to maintain peace. (As mentioned earlier, bonobos are similar to chimpanzees but are a separate species. Their common ancestors split around two million years ago. Socially, bonobos differ fundamentally from chimpanzees. Bonobo females are dominant over males and bonobos are more peaceful. Bonobos live only south of the Congo River. Their range, far smaller than that of their closest relatives, does not overlap with that of chimpanzees.) If the science of watching animals has one great message for humankind, it's that female power—bonobos, elephants, sperm and orca whales, lemurs—tends to create space for peace.

On patrol

❧ ❧ ❧

A while later, we've followed several chimps to the water. It's the dry season and only a little water seeps into a ravine. Sudden commotion marks the arrival of Talisker. He rattles vines and drags his knuckles loudly through the dry leaves. Talisker holds an odd position; he's high ranking but stays outside the power struggles. Talisker is in his mid-forties (nearly twice Ben's age). He might have been the alpha male before Cat started her research project. He's big, with longish hair, and Cat considers him "the best-looking chimp in Waibira." That is saying a lot for a senior citizen who no longer shows the buff muscle of prime-age males. He carries himself as if he doesn't worry. He maintains his status without competing.

Talisker begins enjoying a drink by dipping a wadded up "leaf-sponge." Talisker is an unusual chimpanzee. But he's not a saint. When Rita, who is about thirty years old, approaches the puddle, she pant-grunts to acknowledge his rank. Fear-smiling with lips back and teeth together, she emits a brief, soft scream. Her thirst seems urgent. She reaches out with her right arm and presents her wrist. She's recognized his status; that's all he really wants. But he doesn't move. Then Talisker shoos her off with an emphatic flick of his imperial wrist.

Cat interprets, "She's saying I respect you, I respect you; but I need a drink right now. There's enough water for them both. But he's being a bit of a jerk about it."

Rita goes to Alf. He's also hogging a good little drinking spot. Rita pays her respects. Alf leans back to make room. Rita finally gets herself a long, deep drink. Both Alf and Talisker clearly understand what Rita wants, but Alf is being more of a friend about it. Rita is about eight years older than Alf, but she's fourteen years younger than Talisker. Perhaps a little seniority helps her with Alf. But perhaps it's just personality. Alf is a rather mellow fellow.

We follow Talisker into the forest. Along the trail is a surprisingly relaxed-looking Ben—reining emperor of Waibira—reclining, propped on an elbow. Talisker sits down about twenty paces away, as if for no particular reason, as if he simply feels like sitting here.

Talisker

Ben begins making exaggerated scratching motions along his arm. Talisker does exactly the same. Each scratches, looks at the other, and waits for a response. They are each trying to convince the other to be the one who moves closer and starts grooming. The one who moves shows that he accepts and acknowledges that he is lower ranking.

In his unique position, Talisker does not challenge Ben. But Talisker seldom acknowledges Ben's superior rank.

Ben gives a loud scratch. Talisker gives a scratch, shifts position, and yawns. Cat calls these ego contests "scratch-offs." Talisker looks everywhere except at Ben.

Ben moves about half the distance to Talisker and really sits down—bang!—in his line of sight, making his point clearly and insistently. If Talisker doesn't *clearly* respond, "Then he'll undeniably be ignoring the alpha male."

Talisker seems satisfied that Ben moved closer to him, so he gets up and closes the remaining gap. And—though it would be more "proper" for the lower-ranking Talisker to begin grooming first, they make contact with each other in the same instant. Thus begins their grooming, as if they're the best of friends.

Life for a male chimp is full of politics. Zefa was the second-ranking male—the closest ally—of the previous two alphas in Sonso, Duane and Nick. The first inkling Cat had that Nick's situation was getting a little rocky was when Zefa began buddying up to the likely challenger, Musa. Musa is a big, no-nonsense male who carries an air of authority. Musa *looks* like he should be alpha. Nick lost his alpha status a few months later. But the takeover became a running struggle between two fairly evenly matched males, Musa and Hawa. Hawa won and became alpha—surprising Zefa and everyone else.

From left: *Hawa, Musa, Simon*

For the first time in about twenty years, Zefa had miscalculated. The cost was immediate. He dropped rapidly down the ranks, having to pant-grunt to young males he wouldn't have even bothered to acknowledge a few years earlier. Zefa had followed a clear and sensible strategy. But he'd bet wrong.

Different alphas have different leadership styles. "Their career depends," says Cat, "not just on what they are. It depends on *how* they are." Some top males are very domineering. Some interact mostly with males. Some with males and females.

Good leaders keep their top spots longer. When they fall they don't fall as hard or as far. Of the former Sonso alpha Nick, Cat says with brutal frankness, "He was not a very good chimpanzee." He'd create disputes and conflict.

A field assistant who watched Nick grow up says that Nick was always getting beaten up, and that because he was bullied he became a bully. Even in chimpanzees, apparently, abuse can perpetuate abuse and lead to a kind of toxic masculinity.

"Nick was a terrible, terrible alpha," Cat is saying. No one likes a bully. So Nick didn't hold the alpha position for very long. Often, when a chimp loses his alpha status his position in the hierarchy drops to second or third. Nick's plummeted. "Straight down. And everybody made sure he knew it." He soon died.

PEACE

THREE

A FOREST AT DAWN CAN seem like the quietest place on Earth. Quiet is not the absence of sound. It's the absence of noise. The birds remind us that dawn is the song that quiet sings. In a forest, you can still hear the magic. As daybreak rolls endlessly across the planet, a chorus of birds and monkeys is eternally greeting a new dawn.

On this new morning, Ben and Talisker—whom Cat refers to as "the big boys"—are not with the first group we've found. And now Macallan, age twenty, performs a bit of male bluster, dragging stuff around. But he's almost entirely silent about it. He wants to impress onlookers without summoning Ben's rage.

The performance agitates the females, who'd been restfully eating. One female screams.

Her scream brings Ben suddenly barreling through to make everyone knows who's boss. Now Ben and Macallan are streaking through the trees and then racing across the ground at top speed. Macallan's wails are audible for the next hundred yards.

Ben comes running back, demonstrating authority in all directions, hooting, jumping around trunk to trunk, shaking branches, running in big circles. His performance sends more onlooking chimps up trees, with much agitated *waah*-ing and *aah*-ing.

Satisfied with himself, Ben sits with a regal air.

To be honest, it's all getting on my nerves. The males' demands for acknowledgment of rank, the intimidated screaming and submissive grunting; the young and the females caught in cross-firing ambitions and in the obsessive insecurities of high-status males—it's wearing thin on me. It doesn't just waste everyone's time; it's *oppressive*.

"They make their lives much more unpleasant than necessary," I venture.

"Yeah," sighs Cat.

"It's like living in a gang," I say.

Virtually all the problems chimps create for themselves are caused by male aggression driven by male obsession with male status. Caught in a social web of inflicted ambition, suppression, forced respect, coercion, intergroup violence, and episodic deadly violence within their own community, chimps are their own worst enemies.

Birds and mammals that I've studied defend their nests, their mates, their territories. But no other creature that I've studied has impressed me as *vain*. Chimps are vain. And the vanity of chimps—is male.

Quite simply, it's too familiar. You can see in so many ways that chimps are our close relatives. Chimp male status is gained, lost, and enforced through threats and violence. With chimps as with humans, male passions don't just waste everyone's time; they waste potential for better-quality time.

Testosterone, oxytocin, and cortisone are three main hormones that help create mood and motivation. They help govern aggression, bonding, and stress. Most other animals share these same hormones. Chimps have them. We have them. That's one reason we easily recognize drives and emotions similar to our own in many species. We all know the feelings.

The tedious ridiculousness of chimp male dominance highlights the tedious ridiculousness of the dominance obsessions of too many human males. It's the testosterone talking. Chimps' displays of maleness-for-the-sake-of-it make them—and everyone else—victims of male hormones.

Chimps horrify and delight us because we recognize in them parts of ourselves. We see in them aspects of our own passions and they hold us in fascination. We cannot look away. So much of what is uncomfortable for us in watching chimps is their excruciating similarity to us. The chimps are brutal, imperfect, often insensitive. So are many people.

Violence *within the community* is a defining quirk of chimp life. Humans share that kink. Chimpanzees and humans are the only primates that make tools *and* hunt in groups for meat *and* engage in community-against-community warfare *and* sometimes kill individuals inside their own social groups whom they know well.

Killer whales, sperm whales, elephants, and wolves showcase pinnacles of animal weaponry, power, and intellect. But they do not kill members of their own group. The group exists because all benefit through mutual cooperation in food finding, child support, and defense. But in order to win in chimpanzee society, someone must lose. The difference between those other animals and chimpanzees is like the difference between musical groups and sports teams: In one system everybody wins; in the other someone loses.

Why can't chimpanzees just be nice? Why can't we? Because we're not bonobos. And that's just bad luck. We are as closely related to bonobos as to chimpanzees. Among chimps, humans, and bonobos, some of the thinking is similar, some of the fears and ambitions and emotions the same. But in bonobos the highest-ranking individual is always a female.

Dominance by females makes a big difference for them, because female dominance differs from male dominance. The emphasis in bonobo society surpasses both chimpanzees and humans in creating and maintaining the peace. Among bonobos, fighting is rare; murder is unknown. In the bonobo brain, the areas that perceive distress in other individuals and those that dampen aggressive impulses are enlarged. "The bonobo may well have the most empathic brain of all hominids, including us," writes the primatologist Frans de Waal.

Bonobo females form alliances to keep male aggression in check, preempting violence. By comparison, chimpanzee males form alliances and maintain dominance with violence. In experiments, bonobos unlock doors to eat with strangers, even when it means being outnumbered by members of another group. No chimp would ever do that. Chimpanzees fear and attack strangers. Bonobos will even let a stranger get into a food-filled room that they themselves cannot get into.

Bonobos have been said to have a threefold path to peace:

little violence among males, between sexes, and among communities. The only person who has studied *both* free-living chimps and bonobos, Takeshi Furuichi, has noted that the difference is striking, "With bonobos everything is peaceful," he has said. "When I see bonobos, they seem to be enjoying their lives."

Led by alpha females, bonobos do quite nicely. Why do chimps have alpha *males*? No one knows with certainty how each species got to be the way they are. The full answer probably isn't simple. But perhaps part of the answer is, chimpanzees have alpha males because: They just do. Perhaps male aggression created a self-perpetuating system chimps simply got stuck with. Bonobos don't have that system. Gorillas don't have it. Orangutans don't.

Gorillas live in small groups with one adult male. Different gorilla groups move about in the same area, simply avoiding each other. Orangutans generally mind their own business in relative solitude. Compared to gorillas, bonobos, and orangs, we humans are more socially aggressive, more violent, more vain, more political, more irrationally driven, more prone to escalation through sheer emotion.

We aren't "like apes." We are like *chimpanzees*. Chimpanzees are obsessed with dominance and status within their group; we are obsessed with dominance and status within our group. Chimpanzees oppress within their group; we oppress within our group. Chimpanzee males may turn on their friends and beat their mates; human males may turn on their friends and beat their mates. Chimpanzees and humans are the only two ape species stuck dealing with familiar males who turn dangerous. It's a kind of toxic masculinity. Chimpanzees don't create a safe space; they create a stressful, tension-bound, politically encumbered social world for themselves to inhabit. Which is what we do. This behavioral package exists *only* in chimpanzees and humans.

We often welcome and aid strangers, but we also fear and harm strangers. We feel most friendly toward those who share our group identity and we obsess about emphasizing group differences—with flags, teams, club insignias, funny hats, special songs, and so on. More important than the "origins of human tool use" or of "language," chimps may hold clues to the origins of human irrationality, group hysteria, and political strongmen. Can we recognize a bit of ourselves in chimps' trivial, overly dramatic ambitions? Do they have to be living lives of self-induced stress? Other species' relative peacefulness shows that chimps don't have to be creating such stress for themselves. We don't have to, either. Yet we do.

Of course, many humans control their impulses, and some, magnificently, even work for a better world. That's *also* who we are. Yet if you look at what we do to the rest of the living world and too often to other people, our better selves don't seem generally in command. That's why we have such problems.

Why—for chimps and for us—must this be so hard? Something better is possible. Other creatures have done the experiment for us. All the other apes, plus elephants and wolves, orca and sperm whales, lemurs, hyenas; they show us a path to being better people. Their conclusion: It isn't necessary to be so nasty to those you know, those in your own community. Being nice, being supportive—that can work. It works better.

In elephants and killer whales and some others, as we've discussed, status comes with maturity; no violence is involved, no elder gets deposed. Individuals ascend to leadership with the wisdom of age because their knowledge is valuable. Most such species happen to live, as do bonobos, in female-led groups. Their societies emphasize social support.

Although other species show us all that there are different, better, less stressful, less obsessive-compulsive ways to earn leadership, for chimpanzees the way it is is simply the way it is. This must be a cautionary tale for those of us who'd like to move humankind off our square. Our inability to conquer violence is frustrating. But we have the ability to recognize that it's a problem. From that capacity springs our eternal hope. Chimpanzees seem to have trapped themselves in a more violent society than was necessary.

It's been another difficult day of hard bushwhacking through thick vegetation, more than once following chimps on hands and knees. On the long walk home to camp, there's plenty of time to talk.

Why, I am asking Cat, are chimpanzees so obsessed with male advantage? When other species have found a more peaceful path, why do chimpanzees create so much nastiness?

"I'm afraid you've gotten a skewed view of male aggression," Cat offers diplomatically. "What you're seeing isn't what the majority of chimp life is like." Cat explains that because it's the dry season, fruit trees are loaded with food, so more chimps are spending more time together in larger groups. Larger groups spark more interactions. More excitability. "Plenty of food and plenty of action," Cat sums up. In the rainy season there's less food, and it's more scattered. Chimps spread out and parties are much smaller. Life is quieter then.

She says, too, that we've been following males. Males go where there are other males, and males generate most of the drama. If we'd been following mainly females, we'd see where the peace resides.

In a chimp community it's normal for adult females to greatly outnumber adult males because males die at a higher rate, largely from infected fight wounds. That's how it is in Sonso—about two females to every male. But Waibira, Cat says, "is radically different; it's just boys, boys, boys." Waibira has a nearly even ratio of adult males and adult females, around thirty of each. You'd think a lot of males would mean a lot of fights. But it's the opposite.

"Because there are so many big boys, getting into a fight is now extremely risky," Cat explains. "So in Waibira it's more like 'use your words, not your fists.'" Life for males in Waibira," she notes, is "much more gestural." More signaling, less fighting. "Waibira chimps have a different style of male interaction."

A style is a way of doing something that ripples through a community. Chimps have styles. Perhaps it could be said that cultures are made of styles.

I'm seeing that there are great ironies within chimpanzee life. It *looks* as though being top male is what everyone should want to be. But the benefits are unclear. It *looks* as though males, with their blustery displays, are obsessed with status. But some, calling little attention to themselves, subtly opt for a peaceful path outside the politics. It *looks* as though males create unnecessary violence. But here in Waibira, restraint avoids violence and helps keep the peace.

PEACE

FOUR

CHIMPANZEES ARE FAMOUS TOOL USERS. We now know of various toolmakers and users across a wide spectrum: monkeys, sea otters, wrasse fish, and vultures who use stones to crack nuts, shellfish, and eggs; herons who use bait to lure fish; finches and parrots who make insect probes. There are dolphins who use sponges to glove their snouts. And even ants who use leaves and soft wood to sop up liquid food, and wasps who seal victims in by dropping pebbles into holes and then pounding them in place. And those are just a few.

Most chimps forage for termites with a single tool. But in a place called Goualougo they prepare a two-tool set, one to puncture a termite tunnel, then a finer tool for extracting termites. In a couple of places chimps use sticks for breaking into termite mounds, or to dip into a swarm of army ants. (They swipe the angry ants off the wand and quickly shove them into their mouths, crunching them before they get much chance to bite back.) Others use sticks for digging tubers. In one group at Tanzania's famed

Gombe National Park, young chimps even use sticks to tickle themselves.

Chimps also use stick tools to get honey. A love of honey, and the use of sticks to get it, is another thing we share. When I was in my twenties in Kenya, my new Maasai friend Moses Kipelian showed me how his people dig honey from underground hives of stingless bees. He used two tools: a stout digging stick and a more slender stick. Similarly, chimps not far from Budongo, in Bulindi, get honey from stingless bees nesting underground by using digging sticks to get into the underground nests, then switching to delicate probes. To get into beehives in the hollow branches of high trees, some honey-seeking chimps use a variety of tools in sequence, a "pounder," "perforator," "enlarger," and "collector." They first pound their way into the entrance with a stout branch, then use thinner sticks to open up access to deep combs filled with honey and larvae, and then probe out honey with even smaller sticks. At one tree, researchers found about a hundred such tools.

Like humans, chimps make different tools in different places. Chimps here in Budongo Forest—*unlike* chimps everywhere else—don't use sticks or wood tools for food getting. This might be because Budongo is rich in fruit. Chimpanzees of the northern Democratic Republic of the Congo have a diverse culture of tools and customs. They use long probes of well over a meter in length to get driver ants, short probes for ants of other types and for stingless bees, thin wands for honey in tree nests, and digging sticks for underground bee nests. They pound open African giant snails, tortoises, and certain termite mounds that chimps in most other regions ignore. And they often make their sleeping nests on the ground. In Congo they make nearly thirty different tools. Chimpanzees' total toolkit as a species includes various kinds of probes, hammers, anvils, clubs, sponges, leaf seats, fly whisks, and other gadgets.

The point is, chimpanzees in different places have differing material and behavioral cultures. Even in adjacent communities where the same plants grow, chimps of one community customarily make longer and wider tools than their neighbors.

After Jane Goodall became famous for discovering that chimpanzees use stick tools, West African chimps' use of stones for nut cracking was rediscovered. "At the base of several species of fruit trees that drop hard-shelled nuts," wrote one researcher, "the chimps gathered to create workshops."

Only in West Africa west of the Sassandra-N'Zo River, apparently, do chimpanzees crack nuts with stones. For those groups that do crack nuts, which nuts they choose, how they learn to crack them, and which tools they learn to choose varies culturally from population to population. Thus, some are said to have "nut-cracking traditions."

Cracking different nuts requires a set of skills because different nuts vary in hardness and shape. Nut-cracking chimps consider the type of nut, then, based on experience, select a tool for the task. For softer nuts, they may choose wood clubs; the hardest nuts require stones. A chimp carefully places a nut into, say, a depression in an exposed tree root, then strikes it with a stone or club. Some arrange a stone as an anvil upon which to hammer the nut with another stone. Sometimes a third stone angles the anvil. (Anvils weigh five to six pounds; hammer stones are around two pounds.) A chimp must strike precisely or the nut can jump away when hit. Sufficient force must crack the shell, but not pulverize the nut. In some places stones are sparse, so the chimps carry them from one cracking site to another. If the nuts they're headed for are far away, they may opt to carry a lighter wooden tool.

Between the ages of three and five years, an infant watches their mother's cracking techniques. In the Republic of Côte d'Ivoire's Taï Forest, chimpanzee mothers sometimes actually guide their child's nut-cracking efforts until they succeed. By about ten years old, highly skilled individuals get the whole nut in just a couple of hammer blows. But some chimps never get the hang; they become what researchers described as "habitual scroungers of others' abandoned half-cracked nuts." Female chimpanzees learn tool use faster and are simply better at it, on average, than males, because male youngsters get more preoccupied with socializing.

Researchers have identified about forty tool-use behaviors culturally learned from other chimps (and in orangutans, nineteen). Orangutans are adept with their own tools, using leaves as hand protectors, face wipes, and seat cushions; making protective awnings over their nests; even using wood implements to masturbate. In captivity, orangutans have made wire tools for opening door jambs—and then hidden them, keeping befuddled zookeepers mystified about how they kept getting out. I've seen captive orangs string up their own hammocks. I watched one put on a T-shirt prior to napping. After she woke, I watched her tear a strip off a piece of cloth, use it to string wooden beads, knot the ends, and wear her new crown. The keeper swore no one taught her that. This wasn't just thinking ahead and envisioning an outcome, it was also body ornamenting, a self-concept with an aesthetic flourish. Gorillas rarely use an implement. Nor do free-living bonobos—which is odd because in captivity bonobos use tools just fine.

Animals are born genetically enabled to perform or learn certain behaviors, including the traditions of our tribe. But not everyone, everywhere, learns everything. Although chimpanzees in East Africa do not crack nuts, East African chimps brought into a sanctuary with skilled West African nut crackers easily learn by observation how to use stones as hammers and anvils. The East Africans have the *capacity*. They don't have the *custom*. They can acquire the custom. That's what culture is about.

❧ ❧ ❧

Today we've followed the chimps on their daily trek to the waterholes. It's called the dry season for a reason, and thirsty chimps crowd the shrinking drinking spots. However, one adult, Onyofi, has innovated a way to get clean water. Using her left hand and some determination, she rakes a shallow well and waits while it fills. (Onyofi's name means "finger." Her right index finger sticks straight out from a paralyzed hand.)

Everyone around has been watching Onyofi, interested in what she's doing. One of the babies imitates her digging. He doesn't seem to know why, other than that he's doing something a grownup is doing.

Next, Onyofi takes a handful of leaves, chews them into a wad, takes the wad from her mouth, then dips this "leaf sponge" into her well. She brings it dripping into her mouth, presses the water out with her tongue, savors the private drink that her work has earned, and repeats.

Twenty-year-old Tibu also digs a shallow well and makes a leaf sponge. Tibu's little one begs for her mother's leaf sponge, poking it and touching her own mouth.

Young chimps often sponge drink alongside their mothers. That's hardly surprising; they do *everything* alongside their mothers. What must a chimp learn by watching other chimps? Put it this way: They must learn *everything*. Their long childhood, like ours, is for learning how to become who they will be. They must *learn* how to be normal. Theirs is a wild life that is also a cultured existence.

A little chimp begins learning their culture by watching their mother. In a food tree, an adult might have a ring of juveniles closely observing them eating, often so close that they're right in their face. In populations where they probe for termites or use tools to crack nuts, a youngster learns their mother's techniques.

And as we've seen, all their social etiquette—who gets respect, who gets snubbed—must also be *learned*. Cat says, "They're not *born* political. That side emerges as they learn to navigate the social world. Their more basic instinct is to be curious, make friends with everyone, and be positive," says Cat. "You learn the rest later."

Among animals generally, the importance of mothers in learning is underappreciated because, well, who has time to watch thousands of species growing up?

Grizzly bear expert Barrie Gilbert got to know a female who fished for salmon at Alaska's McNeil River by standing on a couple of particular rocks with her paw cocked in a certain way so she could swat leaping fish. Her youngster learned exactly the same stance. Black bear expert Ben Kilham has raised and rewilded hundreds of orphaned cubs. When I visited him in New Hampshire one cub-filled spring, he explained that the cubs' genes give them all the things needed to survive in their world—but they need an opportunity to learn *how*. That opportunity is their mother. The mother leads them through a complex physical and social environment, keeping them safe while introducing them to all the foods, situations, and dangers they'll need to know about. "If you go out walking with cubs," Ben elaborates, "you see that they want information." Some plants are poisonous; how do they learn what's good?

Ben did an experiment. He knew the tiny cubs he was out with had never eaten red clover. "So I found some, bent down, put it in my mouth. They rushed over and stuck their noses in my mouth, smelling. Then they immediately went searching for whatever smelled like what I was eating, and found some red clover and ate it. This is how they socially learn foods, from their mother." He added, "We had a young cub, Teddy, who hadn't eaten jack-in-the-pulpit even though it's a food that bears eat regularly." An older bear named Curls came around and was eating jack-in-the-pulpit. "Teddy followed her, sniffing in all the holes where Curls had pulled a plant. Then he found some growing, and started eating. This is all *social* learning," Kilham emphasized, "but books tell you bears are solitary."

Perhaps the most bizarre example of the young picking up adult culture from parents—and therefore the most instructively eye-opening—is the very strange case of the mallard duckling who was adopted by loons and did some very un-mallard-like purely loony things. Mallards *never* ride on their parents' backs (loons do, and this adopted mallard did); mallards *never* dive underwater (loons do, and this adopted mallard did); mallards *never* catch fish (loons do, and this adopted mallard ate the fish its loon-parents fed it). When a nice, normal loon family has a nice, normal chick or two riding around, diving, and eating fish, we assume chicks ride parents by "instinct," dive by "instinct," and eat fish simply because that's loon for "dinner." It takes a wayward duckling in an alien family to give us a whiff of how much cultural learning goes on, and how much flexibility exists at each step of the way in becoming wild.

When spotted dolphin mothers hunt alone, chasing a fish usually takes less than three seconds. But when foraging with youngsters under three years old, they often let chasing go on for half a minute, sometimes repeatedly releasing and catching a fish to prompt the young to participate in chasing. Various cats, from house cats to cheetahs, jaguars to tigers, release live prey near their young ones. Orca (killer) whales sometimes stun prey for young ones with their tails or toss prey to them.

So if you're an infant chimpanzee, you go with the group on a particular trail to a particular tree. Now you know where the tree is. You'll learn what the food looks and smells like when it's ready. You'll feel the season when it's ripe. And you know where water is, and how to make sponges that are especially helpful in the dry season. Alone, you would not know. But now you know, because you got led here as a child. You saw others do it. You've learned "how we do things"—your culture.

To learn is to become. Some animals cannot "become" without a social group. A honeybee cannot be a honeybee without being a member of a colony in a hive. A human in isolation cannot be human. A chimp alone is not a chimp; chimps need chimpanzee society. Social animals must live in, be part of, and help create their appropriate social context or they cannot be, or learn to become, who they are.

Pascal

When animals move into a new group, they often adopt the customs of the new group. Once, a tuberculosis outbreak killed half the males in a well-studied group of savanna baboons. The most aggressive males died, leaving as survivors an unusually non-aggressive group. A decade later, after all the males who had lived through the outbreak had died off, this peaceful era persisted. In this species, adolescent males leave the group they were born into and take up life in a new group. Even though new immigrant males had grown up among typically aggressive male role models in their birth group, when they arrived in the placid troop they adopted its uniquely laid-back culture, including high grooming rates between females and males and a "relaxed" hierarchy.

We've said that culture is "how we do things." But that definition leaves out *innovators*, the most important, rarest—and the most resisted—creators of culture. In 1953 (before formal studies of free-living creatures' behaviors), one female Japanese macaque named Imo started washing sand and dirt off of potatoes that people had given to her group. Her innovation spread to kin and to playmates. She became famous as the first known other-than-human cultural innovator.

There is no culture without innovators who do something new. Intelligence can be understood as the ability to do something new. Yet *culture* is mainly about conformity, consistency, and tradition—doing what everyone else does. The fact is, culture requires *both* innovators who create some new thing and adopters who, by learning, narrow themselves and conform. Being conservative is safer than being free-thinking. Safer than experimenting and innovating. Yet without free thinkers and innovators, nothing ever improves, no one adjusts to change, and no culture *ever* arises.

All chimpanzee groups do some hunting of monkeys and small forest antelopes. One group makes dagger-like hunting weapons that they thrust into tree holes to hunt small primates called bush babies. We might see weapons as an *advance*. In one sense, sure, a technological advance. But there are other ways to express intellect. For instance, an advance of emotional intelligence: superior empathy. When a bush baby got *into* a pen housing rescued gorillas in Cameroon, the gorillas held and petted it, observed it with total fascination, then very carefully carried it to the edge of the pen and released it. (You can see a video of it on the Web; search for "gorilla bush baby.") It's one of the most impressive things I have ever seen. The capacity to exert care and effort so as to cause no harm—that's *quite* an advance.

As the world's main weapon crafters, humans are well qualified to praise weaponizing chimps for "foresight and intellectual complexity," as some researchers wrote. But I find the gorillas' gentleness humbling. It shows foresight and intellectual complexity of an elevated kind. It's something we could look up to and hope to learn from. Many humans inflict worse pain and damage than do the dagger-thrusting chimps. Not many humans are any gentler than the gorillas.

What would the world be like if the "early human relatives" who would evolve into the planet's most dominating, devastating toolmaker had brought with them instead a disposition that walked a more peaceful path, less like that of a chimpanzee, more like that of a gorilla or bonobo?

PEACE

FIVE

SOME OF THE THINGS THAT chimps communicate with gestures include: "Let's make contact," "Give me that," "Follow me," "Let's travel," "Move closer to me," "Move away from me," "Look here," "Stop that," "Climb on me," "Let me climb on you," "Let's groom," "Reposition yourself," "Focus your grooming on this spot," "Pick me up," "Let's play."

Why don't they just talk? Chimpanzees and humans have different versions of the gene called FOXP2, which affects the ability to articulate speech. Chimps lack fine control of their vocal cords. Having something to say but not being able to say it might be why gesturing is a major component of chimp communication.

All apes use gestures. That includes humans. Gesture becomes communication when it's directed at a specific individual, who changes their behavior in response. Sometimes you see the gesturer persisting by repeating, or trying something new to get a reaction. Budongo chimps collectively use at least sixty-six different intentional gestures. Of these, about thirty get used regularly.

As each of us doesn't use all the words in our language, any particular individual chimpanzee uses only around fifteen to twenty gestures out of the regional repertoire. Gorillas have a total repertoire of 102 gesture types. (Apes are not alone in using gestures. Ravens gesture to direct the attention of other ravens. Dogs use a total of at least nineteen gestures to get a point across to humans.)

Chimps gesture frequently. Tapping someone with a branch, or swinging an arm or a leg, or a c'mon-style wave of a hand, can all mean "Follow me."

A human word can mean different things, depending on context. The English word "Hey!" can be a friendly greeting or a hostile warning. We understand the user's intent because we understand context. For chimpanzees, a scratch can mean "come closer," let's groom. But when it's obvious that you're leaving, a "come closer" scratch is an invitation to follow. "Stop that" is a slap on the ground, but other gestures mean the same thing. Cat explains, "You'd tell a high-ranking male to stop in a different way than you'd want to tell your mother or your kid."

If their hand is held vertically, like a human about to shake hands with someone, it's usually for friendly contact. If you extend your arm like that but your fingers are curled in, it's usually because you're greeting someone high-ranking and you're nervous about your vulnerable fingers.

A bare-teeth grin usually indicates nervousness. Its message is: 'Look, my teeth are closed; my jaws are not opened to bite. I will not be attacking you; I am safe and I regard and approach you with peaceful intent.' The human greeting smile—the assurance that we intend friendliness, especially to a stranger—originated in this "bare-teeth grin" that communicates peaceful intent.

Chimps beg—for meat, for fruit, for sponges—with an open hand with upturned palm. It's our beg, too; we likely inherited it from our common ancestor. Human toddlers use fifty-two distinct gestures, and chimpanzees use forty-six of those *same* gestures—a 90 percent overlap. At least thirty-six specific gestures are shared among *all* of the nonhuman great apes.

This overlap suggests that we all—all the apes, including humans—inherited from an older common ancestor the ability to create, learn, and use these ancient packets of meaning, signals that have been flashed through Africa's forests for millions of years.

To really see how an ape thinks, you have to see communication *failing*. If a captive orangutan, for instance, is trying to get a banana but a human offers a cucumber—the orang will try a totally different signal. But if the human is close to getting it—offering one banana from a bunch when the orangutan wants the bunch—the orang will keep repeating the same cue. When someone is far from getting it, you switch your cue; when their guesses are close to correct, you repeat and intensify the same cue. This to how humans play charades.

Humans are incessant talkers. We even have sign languages consisting entirely of gestures. So communicating without language seems a surprising proposition. But let's not underestimate the power of simple gestures. Opening our arms to offer a hug is not language. But it communicates a profound message.

People say that you can't think without language. Other creatures show how it's done.

When a raven call signifies "Food here" to their friends, they show us their thoughts.

"Many people don't consider it language unless the ordering of the parts can change the meaning," Cat acknowledges. (The phrases "a spotted dog" and "a dogged spot" mean different things.) But she observes, "That's important in how humans communicate. It's less important if your goal is to understand how chimpanzees communicate."

I knew Cat and I would get along when she said, "I haven't come to work in a remote Ugandan forest because I am interested in 'how we became toolmakers.' I'm here because I'm interested in chimps."

PEACE

SIX

ONE OF THE CHIMPS AT the waterhole still has a serious-sounding cough. He bends branches into a nest and lies down.

"He must be feeling miserable," Cat comments. When people enter the forest to cut wood or set snares, they sometimes leave plastic cups at waterholes. A curious chimp might pick one up and catch a life-threatening cold virus left by a human hand.

Ten days ago the coughing cold claimed Ketie's two-year-old daughter, Karyo. Ketie is still carrying her daughter's body.

"I think she understands the baby's dead," Cat says. "But ..."

A pitiful sight.

Now three small chimps, apparently newly orphaned, descend the slope—a juvenile boy, and a girl of perhaps six years carrying a young baby. It's likely that these lost children are a brother and sister and their very young sibling. The baby is about a year-and-a-half old—only half the age where survival without milk might be possible. The sister clutches the baby protectively to her body.

The little one, too weak to cling, cries continually. Whatever happened to their mother occurred within the last couple of days.

A baby under five who loses their mother may simply lose the will to live. Ten-year-old Spini and her little four-year-old brother Soldati lost their thirty-year-old mother a few months ago. But their luck is holding. They have been playing with Lotty, Liz, and Monika.

In some cases a close female friend of their deceased mother will adopt an orphan, protecting them during travels, shielding them from conflicts. Some adult males adopt.

PEACE

SEVEN

CHIMPANZEES' CONTAGIOUS EXCITEMENT IS AS obvious as the bright side of the moon. The deeper nature of chimpanzees gets overshadowed, but it includes tender concern for others.

Sometimes acting out of compassion for another's benefit brings chimpanzees into danger. The word for that: altruism. When a companion is unaware of a danger, a chimp is more likely to sound an alarm. In two separate incidents in zoos, a mother and a male chimpanzee drowned while trying to rescue babies who had fallen into motes surrounding their enclosures. Zoo chimps sometimes bring food or even mouthfuls of water to elderly group mates.

In Taï Forest, a male named Porthos, with an adopted baby daughter riding on his back, rushed toward distress screams from a female named Bamu. Five males of an adjacent community had captured her. Bamu had years earlier lost an arm; she was helpless against her attackers. With his adopted baby clinging, Porthos charged the five males so fiercely that he saved Bamu. Porthos had certainly risked his life; that very day those same five intruders killed a male of Porthos and Bamu's community.

Leopards have powerful jaws and eighteen claws. One day, a female chimpanzee was rescuing her small son from a leopard. The leopard attacked her. An adult male chimp rushed immediately to her rescue—and *he* was in turn attacked. Over twenty-five years of observation, researcher Christophe Boesch says such heroic altruism is typical of chimpanzees.

After the rescuing male was injured by that leopard, other chimps in the group cared for him for hours, wiping away blood and cleaning dirt from wounds. Boesch notes, "An injured individual receives support for days. Beyond the bluster of status-seeking lies something much deeper in the chimpanzees' social soul."

We need one another. And sometimes, like chimpanzees rushing to the rescue, we simply understand when someone needs us.

When we brought home our new seven-month-old Aussie shepherd pup, Cady, our six- and seven-year-old pooches Chula and Jude wanted nothing to do with her. One morning after she'd been with us for a month, we were on a beach where we often let them run. We were almost back to our car when Cady decided to turn and run after a dog several hundred yards down the beach. If you want to get a young dog in the habit of following, you have to let them realize that you won't wait for them if they high-tail on you, so I kept walking to the car. Chula and Jude, though, didn't share my training concepts. They stopped about sixty paces from me, looking toward the receding puppy and then at me. I called them. Chula came, slowly. But Jude refused. He sat. I called again. He *laid down*, butt to my direction, facing the bouncing, barking dot down the beach. I kept walking toward the car and glancing over my shoulder. Cady was now running back to us fast enough to complete a three-minute mile. When Cady reached the lying-down Jude, he leaped up and followed her, watchfully bringing up the rear of the entourage. We *all* understood that we belong together now. Jude's no-pup-left-behind policy surprised me. Jude seemed to be implying, "In *our* group this is how *we* do things"—the most fundamental concept in culture. For non-human beings, actions speak.

PEACE
EIGHT

BEN THE ALPHA AND LOTTY the senior female seem absorbed in the mutual pleasures of grooming. But with every distant call, both pause. Monitoring chimp sounds coming from different directions in the forest is their version of scrolling through their social media.

One call gets everyone's attention. It's from the rival chimp community. Lotty leaps up and answers, "*Wah!*" It's highly stressful to be in contact with another community who might be into your territory.

"It's a big group over there," Cat assesses. The party we're with is small.

Most interactions between communities are hostile shout-offs.

But sometimes, it's war. About a tenth of male chimpanzees die in warfare. Surprisingly, death rates due to warfare in many *human* societies have often been twice that.

Lotty had screamed. But it might have been better if Lotty had stayed quiet. All week the Waibira chimps have responded to rivals' calls mostly with silence. "I think many of the males have been too sick to take on the challengers," Cat reiterates. "They just weren't up to a confrontation."

And so: Eastern chimps have pushed into Waibira territory.

There's now less coughing. But Ben is still not entirely well. "If I were Ben and Lotty," Cat projects, "I wouldn't want to act without a lot more of the big boys around me."

Ben and Lotty and the others get up. A little group assembles. With lots of pant-grunts and arm reaches they're checking in with each other. Cat says they're "psyching themselves up a little bit."

Gerald arrives. And Monika. When they all seem to feel they have a sufficient critical mass of males, they simply get up—and go.

They lead us up a steep, rocky pitch to a hill beneath gigantic trees. The undergrowth opens. I wonder aloud what's on their minds.

"If I was a chimp," offers Cat, "I'd be thinking, 'If I'm going to recruit anyone else, I need to do it from this hill. Otherwise, no one behind will hear me.'"

Ben, hair erect and agitated, loudly roars, "*Ahhh. Agghhh. Agghhh. Agghhh.*" It's lower, more aggressive, threatening. Actually a bit frightening. Ben begins charging around, hooting and thumping his feet hard on the boomy buttress roots. He listens. Repeats. He's trying to raise a bigger militia.

Chimps who hear his buttress banging will know it's him. Even *that* is individualized. Cat and our guides know whose drumming they are hearing by sound alone.

Sam arrives, and one-legged Tatu on the crutches of her

long, strong arms. Alf and Lafroig appear. Their silence speaks of apprehension.

Sudden distant drum thumps and hooting ringing through the forest instantly make all the males puff up. The Easterner community is calling from near their shared border.

Now Waibira responds—loudly. "*Woough!*" All join. "*Ooh waagh.*" "*Ouwww.*" "*Whooohh.*" "*Hoo-ahhh, hooohh ahh.*" "*Ahhhh wahhhhh.*" It's saying to the other community, "We are many. We are standing our ground."

Another round of distant calls sets off an absolutely fever-pitched eruption of hooting and shrieking from our group. Throughout all leafy points of the compass, the air reverberates.

Suddenly our chimps are gliding toward the calling Easterners across the sun-dappled forest floor. But they are *quiet*. Audio blackout.

Moving absolutely silently, walking with almost no noise in dry leaves, a long caravan of chimps travels for ten or fifteen minutes on one of the major trails. They seem ready for combat. It *feels* like war.

One of the chimps is so nervous about the prospects for an upcoming encounter that he stops and has diarrhea.

In contrast to their silence, our footsteps are so loud in these dry leaves that we are spoiling whatever element of surprise they might have wanted.

No, Cat says; I have that wrong. Notice, she says: They keep stopping to wait for us. "They're good tool users, and they're using us. The other community is afraid of humans. Just the sound of us will halt their advance. They might even retreat."

One chimp picks up a small stick and pauses to sniff it. The rivals were just here. Now our group moves very much slower, hesitant, hunting for those who may be hunting them.

Masariki flashes a fear face to Gerald. They briefly hug reassurance. Then swiftly hurry to join the others.

Cat says of poor Masariki, "He's probably pretty terrified." They seem frightened by the *thought* of the violence that awaits. There's a lot to worry about. If there is physical fighting, it can be brutal. Chimps can die.

Now all halt. Exquisitely attentive. One stands upright on his legs, putting one hand against a tree trunk, peering ahead. There are brief touches for reassurance. Then all advance, with silence so absolute it feels like everyone is holding their breath.

Shouting from the challenging community accelerates our chimps. Still in silence the Waibirans burst into a running charge.

Contact!

A great racket breaks out, with terrifying roars and thunderous stomping. Ben and Talisker come barreling along in full display. Several chimps show strength by breaking off the biggest branches they can manage, dragging them around, and throwing things in their enemies' direction. Screaming Easterners are streaking in retreat like dark comets, leaving the dense vegetation shaking.

Waibira members are yelling a wide array of hoots, *wah*s, and screams.

Suddenly we realize that four or five female Easterners are silently stranded in trees overhead. Our chimps seem intent on trapping them. This is no game.

But those stranded females are a large enough group to

dissuade the Waibira chimps from risking all-out fighting high in trees. So the Easterners begin working out their escape through the canopy, moving away.

However—one of their females decides to bolt to the ground and make a run for it. Gerald rushes her but fails to grab and tackle her. She escapes.

PEACE

NINE

TODAY WE'RE WITH A GROUP that's resting.

We, too, sit and rest.

"Uh-oh," Cat suddenly says, a bit alarmingly. "It's going to be fluffy chaos."

Chaos?

"We've got all the little ones coming."

Forty-year-old Kidepo arrives, her infant's tiny hands gripping her belly. Ndito-Eve comes with seven-year-old Noah and bouncy two-year-old Nimba. Most chimps have dark eyes, but Ndito-Eve's left eye has the white around the iris—called the sclera—like a human eye, making her gaze quite striking. Bahati strides in with little Brian riding her back. Her little cowboy hops off when she pauses to assess the scene. When he taps her to indicate he'd like to get back up, she dips her shoulder so he can hop on.

Brian and a couple of others start chasing one another up and down vine-tangled trunks, then jump onto Monika, who eagerly rolls around with them, tickling, pulling their feet gently, and making open-mouth contact.

An open mouth with lips covering the teeth is called a play face. "The lips start to get pulled back as they start to laugh," Cat explains. The kids are chuckling, their laughter sounding like rapid panting. Human laughing originates from the rapid play-panting evident in our ape cousins.

Play strengthens bonds, maintains social groups, and aids survival. So play is serious stuff. Many creatures play, and what motivates them in the moment is that they have fun doing so.

But as with human children, chimpanzees sometimes get carried away. It can get rough. When one of the youngsters starts screaming in fear, their mother rushes in, also screaming, to break up the roughhousing. She reprimands the other kid. But that kid's mother objects, and a fight erupts between the mothers. For a few seconds the forest sounds as if the gates of hell have burst open. Chimpanzees fleeing the fighting are streaking off in all directions.

Just when the screaming and hooting escalate to fever intensity, Ursus, a thirty-year-old bear of a chimp, rushes in. With a major display, he seems determined to break up the riot and quell this round of trouble. It works. Ursus has brought calm. Order returns.

Social difficulties are inevitable; restoring peace takes effort and skill. Male chimps can both disturb and restore the peace, be peace breakers and peace brokers. A chimp like Ursus has to understand and want peace, and know how to make it happen.

Ursus is the biggest and strongest guy here at the moment. But he's mellow, not competitive; he doesn't seem to be gunning for alpha. "Maybe he'll do the strategy of 'I'll just hang here with the ladies, father a few children, live a fat and happy long life,'" Cat speculates. Ursus seems to have a way of being male without the drama, deriving respect through seniority. One might say he's earned it rather than won it. He shows that a peaceful path is possible, and that even male chimps can make peace happen.

Meanwhile, four-year-old Nalala is spinning on a vine. His mother, Nora, raises an arm to say "come," and pulls him into her embrace. Their contortions are comic, relaxed. She rolls him onto his back, buries her face in his belly, and plants a series of open-mouth kisses like a human mother blowing raspberries on the belly of a giggling infant.

Nalala means "sleepy." But now he is hungry. It's the dry season, the weaning season. Nalala makes frequent requests to nurse, using strings of gestures between him and his mom. Nalala taps his mother with his foot. Tap tap tap—. He's persisting. But Nora has no milk.

Right now Nora has the look of a mother with an irritated baby. Nalala suddenly erupts into an absolute weaning tantrum, shrieking, hitting, and even slapping Nora in the face.

Nora merely hugs her child closer. This quells his tantrum. Eventually they relax, lying along a thick vine not far off the ground, with him on top of her. Mom wants to nap. He keeps whimpering. Every now and then she opens an eye, then goes back to trying—perhaps pretending—to nap. He pitches a smaller fit, interrupting himself partway through it to see whether his mother is paying any attention, and whether it's worth continuing the performance.

Nora is a confident, socially versatile mother. She's not nervous when she's alone. She also hangs out a lot with big, high-ranking males. That means that from birth Nalala has been building bonds and watching their dynamics. "And *that* means," Cat is telling me as I watch Nalala not-sleeping with his mom, that, "Nalala will be an outstanding contender to become a very high-ranking male."

He's such an innocent and delightful little bundle. It's unpleasant to think of him three decades from now, locked into a lifetime of competitions, fights, and threatening displays of strength. Being female comes with significant drawbacks. But so does being male in a male-dominated world, because to be male is both to be dominated and to incur the costs of dominating. Maybe he'll choose the path of Ursus.

It's hard to predict what his future holds. Chimpanzee lives run a colorful palette. We see that some males prefer a peaceful life and stay out of the political scrambles while others are obsessed with status and strategic alliances. Females are less political and fight less. They form friendships, because it's just better to travel with a friend than alone.

Conflicts within social groups are inevitable, so managing them is crucial for group stability. Intervention by bystanders reflects a sense of community concern that is rare among nonhumans (and not universal in humans). Chimps acting as if fights are "bad" suggests a *sense* of bad and good—a moral nature.

Because conflicts do inevitably arise, reconciliation *after* fights is very important. Sometimes a third chimpanzee will get in the middle of two chimps who need to patch up a fight. The mediator will start to groom one of them, so that soon they are both grooming the mediator. The mediator might then get up and walk away, leaving the combatants in a situation already cooled down by the mediator. Then the combatants will groom each other, smooth things over, and be all right. None of this is accidental. Because it takes effort and a plan, it can only happen if this is their *desired* outcome.

Chimps seem to understand that "love your enemy" is highly practical advice. Such effort is not simply restoring temporary calm. It is a way to set things whole, a way to hit "reset" on group identity and community belonging. So, too, with us. Revenge isn't the only way to settle scores, and it's not the fix that helps everyone. When there's a crack in the social flow there is a need to keep social things social, to heal the harms. Deciding upon forgiveness and offering reconciliation, even aiding those with whom we've had sharp differences: Such pro-social acts let us turn the page, move on, and—most crucially—keep things together.

As the great pioneering anthropologist Margaret Mead identified "reciprocity" as a cornerstone of human society, Frans de Waal has identified "reconciliation" and peacemaking as a cornerstone of life in chimpanzee society. We also see a tendency to forgive in our dogs. They always want to kiss and make up because they know implicitly, deep-down in their core being, that their relationships are everything. The bear expert Ben Kilham has seen reconciliations in dozens of orphaned bears, where squabbles are frequent but the need to maintain a social network is crucial.

Following a fight in a zoo's chimpanzee night quarters, the attacker spent a large part of the day tending his victim's wounds. Such behavior seems to verge on a sense of responsibility, perhaps remorse.

Is guilt, shame, or remorse possible in non-human beings? "What feeds guilt and shame is a desire to belong," writes de Waal. "The greatest underlying worry is rejection by the group."

Group identity—such a fundamental aspect of culture—both enables and results from empathy, altruism, cooperation, and the need to keep things okay. The driving force is the need to make the group continue as a whole, because the benefits of the group are great.

Nora and Nalala

In a rare patch of sunlight striking the forest floor, Nalala climbs onto Nora's shoulders, and they continue. He rides his mother's back through the forest sitting upright, with one leg tucked under him, seeming as comfortable and secure as any kid might, like he's inherited the world.

PEACE

TEN

TODAY WE'RE TAKING A BREAK from the Waibira chimps. We will visit the adjacent chimp community known as Sonso. Sonso's population is about half the size of Waibira's, and its female-to-male ratio is more typical, with roughly two females to every male.

Harriet is here right now with a new seven-month-old baby. Oakland is playing with her bright-faced three-year-old, Ozzie. There's gentle open-mouthed play biting, lots of reassuring arms around the baby.

Young chimpanzees play with crazy energy. But they have a calming effect on adults. Youngsters often bring adults together to join in the play, creating trust, helping maintain community.

The great Musa arrives, but with no display. Melissa is right here with her two-year-old son, Muhumuza. Muhumuza attacks and play-bites Musa. Minutes of rolling, wrestling, and happy grunting ensue. When the baby finally sits up, the lordly Musa pokes him, just to resume the play.

Another adult—this one with a pale face—approaches and lies on her back near the baby, extends a hand, and, when that doesn't work, gives the baby a light tap to tease him into pouncing. Little Muhumuza pounces. The pale-faced provocateur covers her eyes to protect her face while flailing back with one arm at the attacking ball of fluff.

Simon, twenty-five, comes over from where he's been resting and gently grabs and lets go of the baby's feet. It's a tender moment.

Yes, chimps can be violent, impressively so, and the violence can stay with you. "But, y'know," Cat emphasizes, "if a young one has just screamed because a big male has frightened them, the male will sometimes run over and give them a kiss or a hug. That ability to instantly pivot from being huge and scary to incredibly gentle—it's equally impressive."

After the chimps have indulged in a long period of play, the little ones fidget while parents try to nap.

It's all so peaceful.

Chimpanzees, writes Budongo's pioneering researcher Vernon Reynolds, "have evolved a high degree of what can be called social intelligence, involving appeasement, deception, counter-deception, alliance formation, reconciliation after conflicts, and sympathetic consolation for victims of aggression." Theirs, he says, is a "thinking society," based on the intentions, plans, and strategies of its members. These are capacities we share, enabled by brain circuits we share, originating in evolutionary history that we share. Chimpanzees provide both a cautionary tale for how to get it wrong and instructive mentoring for how to bring it back and make it right. Being with chimpanzees creates a swirl of comparisons and assessments. They come up good and bad. So do we. We are the apes who have most intensified the activities of toolmaking, warfare, pursuit of status, oppression. We are as trapped into enforcing and patrolling boundaries as they are. Humans are the most creative and compassionate *and* the most cruel and destructive species.

It is as hard for us to see chimpanzees for who they are as it is to see ourselves as who we are. If we really understood who *we* are and how we might be, we'd see the choice to honor the compassion that is best in us and we'd grow past what is most unfortunate about us. But we'd have to take a really good look in the mirror and decide—as only *humans* might be capable of doing—what kind of beings we want to be.

I've been trying to understand "What are chimpanzees like?" But as Cat has been trying to get me to see, chimps are not "like" one thing, in any one way. Chimpanzee life is many things, in many ways. Human groups differ in their cultures and chimpanzees across Africa differ in theirs. Will chimpanzees survive in a world of more and more humans? The cheering fact is: When people want to, saving species works. Animals just need room to live, in peace.

For two hours, we live among this loveliness of free-living chimpanzees playing with their babies who are learning how to become wild. I am realizing that life for them is peaceful *most* of the time.

When the resting is finished and the chimpanzees begin filtering away, all go to the right except Simon. He gazes down the trail. Then, choosing the road less traveled, he goes left, walking in the opposite direction, marching to his own drum, alone. He continues south, south, south. He's going somewhere, to someone that he has in mind.

PEACE
THE WRAP

CHIMPANZEES ARE WHO THEY ARE. We all have our lim-itations *and* our superlatives. Living with others can bring many benefits. But inevitably it also brings tensions. When chimpanzees have problems with each other, when they let their ambitions run away with them, their screaming and drama can make it seem like chimpanzee society is quite violent. But that's just an impression. And humans don't always get along, either. We still have much too much competition, fighting, appalling warfare, and much too much hostility to those who are a bit different from us—even in our own communities. Scientific data shows that chimpanzees live peacefully 99 percent of the time.

Let their success in peacefulness be a challenge to us. The chimps are the best they can be. The question for us: Are we?

Scarlet macaws usually travel with someone they know well.

REALM TWO:
CREATING BEAUTY

SCARLET MACAWS

Peruvian Amazon

BEAUTY

ONE

TWO SCARLET MACAWS ARE COMPLICATING our attempt to eat breakfast. At the tourist lodge attached to the Tambopata Research Center in the Peruvian Amazon, Tabasco and Inocencio are working the open-air dining area like professionals, flying from rafters to railings to detect any soft spots in the humans' defenses of pancakes, rice, and rolls.

Researcher Don Brightsmith gets up and says to me, "Guard my plate, please." Along with Gaby Vigo-Trauco, Don directs present-day research on the free-living macaws in the surrounding rainforest. Gaby is Peruvian. At the table with us is their daughter, five-year-old Mandylu. Over the course of three years more than twenty years ago, former researchers here rescued about thirty macaw chicks who were having trouble in their nests. The researchers hand-raised them. They were dubbed the "Chicos," the kids. They were never caged. They easily re-wilded, attracted wild-born mates, and acquired nest sites. But they never forgot their roots, and often returned to the research center to pilfer food.

Gaby Vigo-Trauco

Individual macaws can be highly recognizable. Tabasco, twenty-three years old, has one particular feather that always grows in white. He visits the lodge most days. Inocencio is two years older and also visits most mornings. Inocencio has one distinctly almond-shaped eye. The blueness of his blues is deep and intense. On Inocencio the distinctive scarlet macaw's yellow shawl is unusually wide, as if he wears a bright cape. He's heavy, he's big; he struts like a bad guy. But he has his nurturing side; when he was mated to Chuchuy—pronounced *Chew-chewy*—Inocencio, unlike most male macaws, incubated their eggs.

Inocencio and Gaby

A man named Manolo, who brings our breakfast, chases the Chicos energetically with a water-filled spray bottle. The big birds take it in stride. Manolo has other duties; the Chicos have patience. I find fascinating their hybrid personality, wild and tame, harassed and indulged. They have lived long and prospered.

Chuchuy, twenty-four, arrives. She sports a few green feathers in her scarlet head, and her wings are turquoise rather than the blue of most other scarlet macaws.

I rise and ask Gaby if she'd like anything. As she turns to answer, Inocencio crashes into the plate of little Mandylu. Gaby leaps up, waving her arms. She rolls her eyes and explains, "Inocencio targeted her because she is small, you see? And if it's pancakes? He's insane for pancakes, trying, trying—until he gets one. Tabasco is more hesitant. Inocencio, he just goes for it."

Familiar though they are, the Chicos frighten little Mandylu. They are immense at her scale. And fast. And they violate her sense of propriety. "That was *my* pancake," she asserts, tearfully.

I explain that just as she herself saw it and took it from the plate that was placed before her, he sees it exactly the same way. You wanted a pancake and you took one; he wanted a pancake and he took one. To my surprise, Mandylu seems to accept that explanation. "C'mon," I say. "Let's get you another pancake."

Chico pirating breakfast

I have come specifically for the huge, spectacularly colored long-tailed parrots native to Central and South America that are called macaws. "Macaw" sounds like one species; there are about a dozen and a half. Largest of all at more than a meter in length with a four-foot wingspan is the hyacinth macaw that inhabits vast wetlands such as Brazil's Pantanal. The pirates at our breakfast, scarlet macaws, are only slightly smaller.

Macaws are among the roughly 350 parrot species that are with us worldwide. Humans have labeled various other groupings of their order "amazons," "parakeets," "parrotlets," "lorikeets," "lovebirds," "conures," "cockatoos," "cockatiels," and various other appellations including simply "parrot." They are the modern twigs in a brushy evolutionary branching of birds with deep roots. The reptilian ancestors of birds *and* mammals diverged roughly 300 million years ago. One lineage evolved through dinosaurs to become birds. Mammals are not descended from birds. Nor are they more evolved than birds. Our shared ancient ancestors give us many similarities. Our long separate paths give us many differences. Birds recognizable as parrots have been stirring the air for 50 million years. Like all living things, they continue evolving. One thing we share this morning is a fondness for our breakfasts.

Gaby says, "If you offer them wild fruits that they can get in the forest, it's like a joke to them. They toss them. They are like, 'Hey, I can get these anytime.' They like bread."

Tabasco crashes Don's place setting and pinches a piece of sweet cake from the basket. No harm done and Tabasco and I, at least, are fine with this. He sits on the rail and rolls dough balls with his parrot tongue.

Don asks, "Have you ever touched a parrot's tongue? They're soft, and they're dry. Parrots experience a lot of the world with them." At home my wife and I lived for years with a personality-packed little green-cheeked conure named Rosebud who often tested the food on our plates by touching it with her bill. If she liked that, her next step was an exploratory tongue-touch.

Gaby says that Tabasco targets White people's meals. "Almost all the tourists are White. Tabasco knows that if you're White, you're going to be afraid of him and he can land on your table and snatch food. He knows that brown people understand his game."

Carl Safina waiting for macaws

Many parrots are green, basically. Which makes sense. The big macaws, however, are colored like outlandish cornucopias of tropical fruit. Which makes *no* sense. The scarlet macaws look simply unreasonable. They have scarlet heads; their wings and tails are blue and blue-green *and* their identifying feature is the bright yellow shawl splashed across their shoulders. I wonder: Do birds see beauty in their feathers? Do they hear it in their songs?

The bright colors of macaws look beautiful, but their colors aren't there to entertain us. Birds who have bright colors have them because bright colors look beautiful to other birds. The brightest attract the most mates. So birds with bright colors have the most offspring, and those offspring inherit their parents' genes for bright colors. Over many generations, this process has made many kinds of birds very beautiful indeed.

Chuchuy's first mate (she was ten years old) was wholly wild, not a Chico. So was Inocencio's. Following divorces from those firsts, Chuchuy and Inocencio paired. Being a year apart in age, they had not been raised together.

The Chicos helped researchers understand the surprising extent to which individual macaws can have notable personalities and quirks. Ascencio, a red-and-green macaw, so loved to eat a special sweet Christmas bread called panettone that Don once felt forced to hide his box of panettone under their bedcovers before they left the station for a few hours. But—"When we returned, everything was torn up. He found it, and shredded the box."

Gaby adds, "They know everything."

Parrots have been called "the humans of the bird world." By the science and by their behavior, a parrot's mind functions on par with the monkeys who share this forest.

Scala Naturae, "the ladder of life," is an ancient concept originated by Greek philosophers (Plato, Aristotle, and others) and later advanced in Christianity. It put forth the very convenient (for us) and catastrophic (for the rest of the living world) conclusion that rocks are at the bottom, next come plants, then certain better plants with nicer flowers, then lowly animals, followed by more elevated animals, and then atop the ladder: us. For several thousand years, this was presumed to be the natural order of things. Then came modern sciences in the late 1700s and 1800s. Astronomy with telescopes detected evidence of deep time. Geology showed that Earth and the life on it had once been very different from the world we experience, and that the world changes. The study of evolution showed that living things change in nature, similarly to how they change into new varieties under selective breeding by farmers and animal fanciers. These revolutionary investigations forever disrupted our perception of who we are and where we stand. Needless to say, the discovery that humans are not the center of the universe terrified many people. Many remain terrified.

This leaves us with two problems. One, most people, especially in Western cultures, have inhaled Scala Naturae subconsciously. Many assume that humans are the perfect expression that the universe intended. We see the world as ours. We believe that we may act on the world in any way we want, with no responsibility. This leads to our cultural disrespect for the living world. Two, we assume that the more similar other beings are to us, the better they are. We forget that everything alive has made the whole journey with us. Indeed, most have traveled much longer to get here.

Our subconscious acceptance of Scala Naturae is why we are always "surprised" when an elephant rescues her baby, or a wolf uses strategy, or a parrot knows what's going on. The basis for our surprise is our ignorance, our self-isolation, our insecurity, our need to be the best thing that has happened since stars were born.

We might think of a hundred years, or a thousand years, as a long time. Parrots have been perfecting parrot-ness for 50 million years, a span of time essentially impossible for our human minds to really grasp. Through that time they've been continually honing who they are. It's been a long, strange trip. But here we are, all together now.

Iglecita, another scarlet macaw at Tambopata, is tiny for her species. As a chick she almost died. For days, she was very weak. One journal entry on her reads, "I hope Iglecita makes it through the night." She lets only specific people pet her. She usually visits the research center only during breeding season, roughly November to March. But, Gaby says, "We have one volunteer, Sandra, who has been here four times. Three of those times it was May, far outside the breeding season, and Iglecita came. Somehow, Iglecita appears *every time* Sandra is here. Last time, Sandra hadn't been here for three years. Everybody was joking, 'Iglecita's gonna come.' She came!"

When they have trouble, the Chicos come home for help. When one of them got stung badly by bees, she went to the lodge and stayed in the rafters. When another, Avecita, was badly ill with an internal infection, "She arrived so weak that she might have walked here. She was in horrible shape. She spent ten days in the house." She recovered. Don says, "It was another example of them acting on a concept of 'this is a safe place to come when things are going really badly.'"

Parrots are capable of recalling past events, thinking ahead, taking the visual perspective of others, and sometimes creating novel tools to solve problems. Until recently, researchers believed that only humans could do those things. The parrots haven't changed. It's as if we are just waking up from a long journey through space and having a look around at an interesting new planet.

Certain birds rival apes as toolmakers. New Caledonia crows make hooked tools, something even chimpanzees don't do. And they make barbed tools from strips of particular palm leaves, with a thicker end to hold and a narrow tip that's effective for getting insects out of crevices. It's a rare example of "crafting," where it takes several steps to fashion a tool. Juvenile New Caledonia crows stay with their parents for up to two years, learning toolmaking by closely watching. Crows in different areas across New Caledonia make their tools a bit differently, meaning that the species has several cultural traditions. And ravens perform as well as apes and small children in an experimental task designed to test the ability to plan.

In experiments, several macaws and an African gray parrot learned to take a non-edible token instead of food so they could then trade the token for food they liked better. Thus they understand delayed gratification and the value of currency. The macaws were as good at this as chimpanzees. With differently organized brains, birds and mammals have converged on similar capacities. An African gray parrot named Griffin learned the names of shapes of various three-dimensional objects and was able to apply those names to flat drawings of these shapes. Moreover, when most of the flat shape was hidden, Griffin could often still say what shape the partially exposed drawing represented. This shows that parrots can generalize a concept of shapes of real objects and apply them even to partially hidden drawings.

Like chimpanzees, some species of crows, scrub jays, and ravens change their behavior if they want to hide food but realize they're being watched. To see things from another individual's viewpoint, you have to understand that they can understand. You have to realize that they have a mind. Reacting to being watched requires another capacity: a concept of time. You must understand that *in the future* the watcher might steal what you've tried to store. Not long ago, most psychologists believed that only humans understand that others have minds. We are realizing that we share the world with other kinds of minds.

Tabasco first bred at age ten, pairing with a wild bird named Señora Tabasco. She used to visit the lodge with him. One of Tabasco's daughters, named Tambo, nests in a human-made nest box near the lodge. She comes to the lodge in the tradition started by her father. And she has introduced her wild mate, Pata, to the ways of the lodge as well. "Pata acts like a Chico," Gaby tells me. "To Pata everything is new and interesting." One of Chuchuy and Inocencio's wild-reared offspring, ten-year-old Heredero, likewise learned the routine from his parents and visits frequently for a snack. That some of the tameness and food habits of hand-reared macaws get adopted by fully wild mates and the wild partners of their offspring shows how easily and alertly they observe what the other birds know, following cues. Absorbing the local traditions of their kind, even when it's an unnatural habit, comes naturally to them.

They flexibly learn particular ways that make the world work for them. They learn from each other the components of their culture. The Amazon rainforest is one of the planet's most complicated living systems. What they need—food, minerals, water, nest sites, mates, allies, and safety—all occur in different places and at different times. The things that fully wild macaws learn from each other must be much more complex than grabbing dinner rolls and avoiding waiters with spray bottles. But obviously they can learn a wholly artificial way of life, too—if it's to their advantage.

Eyeing Tabasco with a mixture of exasperation and admiration, Gaby says, "He's always calm, never nervous. When Tabasco was young he was always looking for new things. You'd see his face, like, 'Ah! Something new!' He used to do a lot of exploring—and destroying." He's the only one who regularly went into researchers' bedrooms. He still does, but not every day as in the past. "He's no longer as curious," Gaby notes wistfully. "Everything is familiar to him now." Fondly yet matter-of-factly, Gaby adds, "The Chicos have taught me 90 percent of what I know about macaw personalities. Having them around feels like cheating."

✿ ✿ ✿

Macaws take several years to mature and start breeding because they need time to learn how to live. A lot they learn socially; that's their culture. Knowing what you're doing and how you do it is the great ace in the hole of adult animals. Compared to young individuals, adults are better at getting food and avoiding danger. But learning skills takes time, and once skills are learned, individuals become specialists.

Adapting to change often requires specialists. Where I live, herring gulls exploit human-caused changes, but they do so differently from one another. From the same breeding colony, some herring gulls habitually travel out to sea to follow fishing boats for discarded catch while some forage at landfill garbage heaps and others continue traditional natural foraging, hunting for crabs, whelks, and clams. Sea otters learn a foraging specialty from their mother and keep it, lifelong. Shorebirds called oystercatchers specialize in either stabbing or hammering open mussels. Chicks whose parents stab mussels develop the stabbing technique; those whose parents hammer mussels hammer them.

Gaby and Don, with their front-row seat for the Chicos, have been able to see personalities translate into different ways that individuals approach living, and how their wild mates and offspring picked up some of their techniques and tricks. Bird researchers have documented specialists among eagles, penguins, albatrosses, cormorants, murres, oystercatchers, various songbirds, gulls, and many others. When I trained hawks, I saw that individual birds develop particular techniques for particular situations and often become specialized at catching certain prey in certain ways. Only one wolf family in Yellowstone specializes in hunting bison; only one wolf family in Minnesota specializes in fishing. When you learn how to do something from someone, that is what we mean by "culture."

One morning in 1921 in Great Britain, someone opened a door to get the milk that had been delivered and was surprised to discover holes in the foil tops of the bottles. The crime spread, year by year, until, twenty-five years later, milk bottles in roughly thirty towns across the United Kingdom were being pilfered by cream-sipping thieves. The perpetrators: little chickadee-like birds called blue tits. Did one bird figure out how to steal cream, or did each bird figure it out separately? Experiments suggest that birds learn such skills from watching other birds. In many animals, the young, especially young females, appear to be the best learners (probably because young females generally divert less time to squabbling for dominance).

The world is changing very quickly now because we are

changing it. Enclosed shopping malls that are now part of human culture are also part of the culture of urban birds. Pigeons and sparrows have learned to get into malls—sometimes by using motion-sensors to open doors—and forage the floors for crumbs. (I also see them in underground train stations in New York City.) Urban sparrows and finches often bring cigarette butts to their nests; they've somehow discovered that the nicotine kills bugs. (When I raised homing pigeons it was common practice to buy bags of tobacco stems for nesting material, to control lice.) In some places crows drop nuts on roads and wait for them to get run over by cars. In at least one place they do this at intersections, so they can safely walk out and collect their cracked prizes when the light turns red and the cars stop. They've developed answers to the new question, "How can we survive here, in this never-before world?"

The point is, individuals vary, so cultures vary. Cultures evolve and respond to change. And that means: Cultures can be damaged. Can be lost. When populations vanish, traditions that helped birds and other animals survive and adapt also vanish.

Conservation owes much to an important—but still too limited—concept called biodiversity. "Bio" refers to living things and "biodiversity" is a shorthand reference to the diversity of all life on Earth. This simple term helps us organize our thinking. Ecologists usually think of biodiversity as having three main levels: the "genetic diversity" within any particular species; "species diversity," or the number of species in a given region; and "habitat diversity," refer-ring to the diversity of habitat types such as forests, grasslands, coral reefs, sea ice, and so on. But there's a fourth level we are just becoming aware of: cultural diversity. Skills, traditions, and dialects that animals have innovated and passed along culturally are crucial to helping many populations survive.

As human development shrinks habitats into isolated patches, wild populations decline. Cultural attributes such as birds' songs simplify. In a scientific article titled "Erosion of Animal Cultures in Fragmented Landscapes," researchers reported on a songbird that lives in North Africa and Spain, Dupont's lark. The researchers note that for populations of these larks, "isolation is associated with impoverishment" of their vocal vocabulary. In isolated populations, "song repertoires pass through a cultural bottleneck and significantly decline in variety." Unfortunately, isolated larks are not an isolated case. Researchers studying South America's orange-billed sparrow found that sparrow "song complexity"—the number of syllables per song and song length—deteriorated as humans continued whittling that species' forests into smaller fragments. In Australia, a bird called the regent honeyeater has become very scarce due to loss of habitat. It's now so scarce that young males usually do not hear any adult males singing. With no one to learn from, the young males don't learn how to sing correctly. But females want mates who know how to sing. So males who don't know how to sing often don't get a chance to breed. The lack of song learning is breaking down their vocal culture, making the regent honeyeater decline faster.

BEAUTY

TWO

GABY FIRST LEARNED ABOUT PARROT personality as a teenager in Lima, Peru. She acquired two blue-headed *Pionus* parrots. "Malu was friendly—'scratch me'—but not interested in learning. Luis was avid for new tricks, always watching your hand, wanting to learn. Luis was *smart*." He had calls meaning "predator overhead" (including plastic bags in the wind), and "predator on the ground" (usually a neighbor's cat).

Gaby is telling me this as we're walking through the rainforest to one of several scarlet macaw nests she's been monitoring. She's wearing tall rubber boots and camo pants. A kerchief confines her black ponytail.

Hearing about her childhood pets is interesting. But the *forest*.

The forest overwhelms. We are surrounded by walls of green in all directions. From the ferns of the ground to the leafy ceiling of the high canopy, life-forms occupy every level, growing, often competing. Trees with straight dark trunks, spiny trunks, blotchy trunks. Some moss-covered, others vine-laden. Giant fig trees

Enormous fig tree

have head high fin-like buttress roots. Others drop so-called prop roots downward from the trunk like thick supporting cables. Strangler figs climb the trunks of their victims in their initial vinelike sprint for sunlight. Capirona or "naked" trees shirk off the stranglers by shedding bark, a continuous slow-motion scuffle with their attacker. Myriad saplings bide their time in shade, waiting for years until a giant falls and sunlight triggers their one big chance to surge. Trillions of leaves—pointy, round, flat, ridged, fluted. Palms of many kinds. Fruits and nuts and seedpods litter the ground. And all around grows fungi enough to pulverize everything that dies. Meanwhile the vegetation grows the animals. Everywhere bugs and spiders work to pry their living from the world. Ants of many kinds and sizes patrol the forest floor. Their food and work all differ from one another like trade unions in a vast city. Every few minutes some nearby trees get rustled by spider monkeys, howlers, titis, tamarins, capuchins, or squirrel monkeys. Magical morpho butterflies' wings resemble dried leaves when folded in prayerful rest. But when they move they create a shock of beauty as they weave their electric-blue flickers through sunshafts and shadows. This bewildering green blizzard, this remaining piece of the original world, must be the most confusing profusion of vegetative power on Earth, a great megalopolis of lives and of Life.

"I'm sorry," I offer. "What were you saying?"

"Just, my pet parrots when I was a kid—"

"Okay; I heard that part."

"That's all."

We continue, Gaby and I quiet, moving for minutes through the wholly wondrous.

Our destination is a gigantic *Dipteryx* tree. Its massive trunk has hoisted its canopy far above the surrounding forest. Such giants are called "emergent" trees. *Dipteryx* can live a thousand years. Natural nesting cavities in these trees might last decades, perhaps centuries, producing hundreds of scarlet and red-and-green macaws—like feathered fruits of the tree itself. Macaws like to nest in huge *Dipteryx* trees because they offer broad, open views. The birds don't like trees full of vines or low branches that can hide climbing predators.

But humans have heavily targeted *Dipteryx* to use the wood for flooring and also for charcoal. So throughout vast areas, people with chainsaws have sent the great, gnarled, elder giants whose cavities are needed by birds and other animals crashing to the forest floor, taking macaw populations down with them.

When we get to the tree, its silent enormity and motionless power are awe-inducing. Way up in this tree, a good 120 feet or so, sits a large wooden box about four feet high by two feet wide and deep. A giant birdhouse for macaws. Artificial boxes are a partial solution to the housing shortage. Only scarlet macaws readily accept these houses, however. Red-and-greens strongly prefer natural cavities.

This box was Tabasco's nest for nine years. Four years ago he and Señora Tabasco lost possession to this younger pair that nest here now. That means, of course, that besides love, there is fighting among macaws. The new pair then lost it for a year to another pair, then won it back again, showing that the pair bond lasts even through years when the pair has no nest.

Right now the female is in the nest. The male is off somewhere. Yet there are two other macaws in the crown of the same tree. They are preening each other and fooling around. Gaby says, "There is *no way* that the female in the nest doesn't know who these two are. She would not be sleeping." They are probably their kids, last year's young from this nest, visiting. Gaby scrutinizes them in her binoculars and adds, "They have really young faces. The skin is smooth, it's not wrinkly as in old macaws. They are being very vocal. And the mama is sleeping. She'd be looking out of the nest—at the very least—if she didn't know them."

Macaws don't defend food. Many forage in the same tree when fruit is abundant. But macaws do defend—vigorously, violently— nesting sites. They must.

Seldom does a pair find an empty, undefended, and *desirable* nest. That is partly because nest sites are now so few, and partly because birds want proven nests, not just empty holes. Not every hole is equal. There might be a good reason that a vacant hole is vacant. Some cavities that look quite suitable for nesting are accessible to predators. At such a site chicks and eggs will repeatedly disappear. It might be a cavity that looks good but occasionally fills with rainwater.

Some "bad" nests are actually good. One natural nest hollow has bats roosting on its ceiling. The bats poop on the macaws and the whole nest seethes with roaches. Yet it succeeds, and the birds fight over it. The best way for macaws to know if a hole is good is that it's been successful in the most recent season.

This means that most pairs acquire their nest by fighting for it. A good nest, one that fledges chicks every year, gets challenged at least once a season. Challenges are not always violent. The residents' threat calls can be enough for all parties to size each other up. Sometimes, a mere threat and a chase scare away the challengers. If intruders recognize strength in the nest holders, there is no physical contact, no real fighting.

The thing is, they are making crucial assessments of each other. The birds all understand one another's goals; they all know that the challengers are trying to take the site and the nesters are trying to hold on to it. It often appears that they are thinking, making judgments. If a challenging pair detects youth and inexperience, or old age, they may think they have a good chance. And if the nesters have no intention of going quietly, then—the fighting can be brutally violent. A breeder and an intruder may find themselves together inside the nest, fighting violently in confined quarters. The screaming is intense.

Fights usually last hours, often a day. Researchers here have seen breeders at the entrance of the nest for two or three days, fending off repeated takeover attempts.

Several members of Gaby and Don's team are now here beneath the nest in the huge *Dipteryx* tree. One of the team is donning climbing gear. Each day the researchers climb to several nests to check who has hatched and to document chick growth and survival.

As the climber ascends, the agitated female begins growling. She bites the wooden box, showing what that beak can do. Both parents are now present, and very annoyed.

"Last year," Gaby notes by way of contrasts, "we had macaw researchers visiting from Mexico. The poaching for the pet trade there is so bad that in some years, every chick gets stolen from every nest they monitor. So in Mexico, when people show up, the macaws leave. The Mexicans were so surprised at how our macaws stayed, defensive and defiant. I told them, 'Here, we meet as equals.'"

Scarlet macaws live from southern Mexico through Amazonia, one of the largest ranges of any parrot. Being so widespread, they're in no imminent danger of complete extinction. But in many areas scarlets have suffered drastic declines and regional disappearances. Throughout Central America they're endangered.

Worldwide, nearly a third of parrots are already reduced to low or rapidly declining populations. Several have gone extinct in recent times. Farming, logging, the cage-bird trade, killing for the cooking pot, killing by farmers: It all adds up to big troubles for parrots.

The climber is just reaching the nest. It's hot and sticky and buggy down here, but he's feeling the breeze and enjoying a panoramic view of rainforest to the far horizons.

The parents begin screaming. It's high intensity.

The climber has opened the door to the nest and is reaching in. He's met by more than the rich macaw smell. The adult there is lunging at his hand and face.

Gaby adds that the Chicos, having been hand-raised, had no inhibitions about physically attacking researchers at their nests. "It was scary," Gaby recalls. Occasionally a Chico would simply fasten onto a researcher and sink their giant bill—which can easily crack a Brazil nut—into, for instance, a shoulder. "Don can tell you how awful the pain was," Gaby adds. "The females were *really* bad. Especially Chuchuy; at the house you can give her some yogurt and she licks from the cup and you think you are friends. But then you climb her nest and she tries to cut the rope you're climbing."

"And what would she say about you?" I counter, just to tease. "She comes and eats with you and thinks you're her friend—and then you invade her nest, barging in and removing her chicks and handling and weighing them every day. Is that polite? What's a mother to do?"

High above our heads, the researcher puts the large, twenty-five-day-old chick in a bucket that he lowers gently to the ground. He'll wait up there while the team weighs and measures and assesses health. The adults will stay a few feet away, threatening and screaming occasionally. They know the drill; they've been going through this daily since their first egg hatched.

"Know your enemy" is a saying. In a famous series of studies,

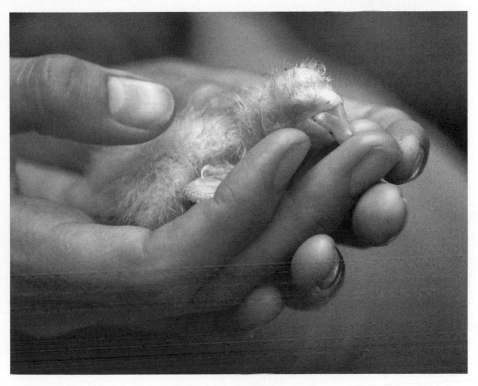

Macaw recently hatched

John Marzluff and his team caught crows so they could tag them with leg bands. After being marked and measured, whenever the crows saw those people walk across the university campus, they'd loudly scold them. Marzluff did not want to upset the crows whenever he and his students strolled the campus, nor did he wish to have indignant crows dive-bombing them wherever they walked. So Marzluff started wearing masks during captures. Nine years later, researchers donned the masks their team wore while catching crows. Crows still reacted to the masks, including crows too young to have been around during the bad old days of captures. Those who'd had the memories of the terror, and the images of their persecutors, had demonstrated to young individuals that these were dangerous folk. The naive ones, having never had a bad experience themselves, learned from elders to harass the masked researchers. As the song says of human children, "You have to be taught to hate and fear." And so with crows. Crows remember good things, too. In fact, a mysterious, almost mystical thing about crows is the many instances of them giving gifts to people who've fed or shown them kindness. Often these gifts are shiny or colorful human-made objects. A culture of fear and a culture of—generosity? Do they *intend* to return a favor? Hard to say with certainty, but it seems so. This might not be culture like humans have. It's culture like crows have.

The angry macaws trying to protect their nest are a hazard for Gaby's climbing assistant, but the ground isn't entirely safe. We watch streams of hunting leaf-cutter and army ants. Leaf-cutters will eat your pack if you leave it. Army ants will eat you. Bullet ants have a bite like slamming a door on your finger. Gliding ants will swarm your pack for its sweat when you leave it. Sweat bees like to swarm your ears and nose. They don't sting. They bite. Once, while a climber was in a tree at a nest, Gaby grabbed a rope—and suddenly got a life-threatening viper bite. The antivenom was at the lodge. She knew she was not "supposed to" run for help; you don't want a racing heart to circulate the venom faster. "What choice did I have?" she asks. Her team met her halfway. She's here telling the tale.

As the bucket reaches the ground, the team veterinarian disinfects her hands to receive the hefty chick. It has several botfly larvae. Botflies can be harmless or can kill chicks, depending on their location. A bit of cream over the entrance to the botfly's burrow in living flesh blocks the larvae's source of air. In a minute the rice-sized maggot tries to come through the hole for a breath. A waiting pair of tweezers ends its picnic. No one feels sorry for the botfly larvae.

Today the team has brought a nineteen-day-old chick to be returned *into* its nest with its twenty-five-day-old sibling who has just been relieved of its botfly. The younger chick had been taken into the lab because the parents were not adequately caring for it. At the research center, this small chick received ten days of intensive feeding and veterinary care. Now though, even at nineteen days, the still-naked chick retains the wobbly and unfocused look of an infant.

Chickens and ducklings hatch with a full coat of down, able to walk, follow their parent, begin learning, and feed themselves. At the other end of the spectrum: parrots. Parrots hatch pink, near-naked, blind, deaf, and helpless. Their closed-up ears and eyes don't open for a couple of weeks, and during that time they look positively *larval*. I've seen many kinds of newly hatched birds: hawks and doves, songbirds and shorebirds, seabirds and others. Some are adorably cute right out of the egg. Parrots—it gives me no joy to say—are the ugliest baby birds I know. It is fit justice that such ugly chicks grow into some of the most beautiful, smartest, personable, calculating birds in the world. But quality takes time. Scarlet macaw chicks grow more slowly than any other parrot. New-hatched scarlets weigh about an ounce, about one thirty-fifth of adult weight. Adults weigh about a kilo, a bit over two pounds.

The ground team places both chicks into the bucket and sends them homeward toward the sky. The waiting climber places them in their nest, then rappels back to earth.

Will the parents accept or ignore the much-smaller second chick?

There's a camera in the nest. Gaby is filled with maternal anxiety as we retreat to where a video monitor is set up under a tarp. Gaby holds a stopwatch and a clipboard and will note all interactions by each adult, and which chick gets fed when, and for how long.

Gaby has done this six times previously. All adults have accepted each newly replaced chick after its prolonged absence. Chicks must consistently gain weight to maintain health. Fifty feedings a day are not unusual. Nesting and chick rearing is a fulltime job. If a chick is to survive, parental attention must be near constant.

Less than five minutes after we've sent the chicks back into the nest, the male arrives. He inspects the larger chick and then grasps the smaller chick's bill and gives a shake, stimulating the chick to open wide. The mandible of a small chick is shaped a bit like two hands begging. It presents a wide feeding target. The male bends his head and quivers as he pumps food into the newly replaced chick. This is a great relief to Gaby.

While this male is feeding, his mate comes into the nest.

As a breeze sways the treetops, Gaby says cheerfully, "It's a rock-a-bye moment."

Soon this female gives the smaller chick a feeding so prolonged that Gaby, fixated wide-eyed on the black-and-white monitor, says, "My goodness. Gonna make it pop."

The larger chick gets fed, too. Then the mother preens the chicks for minutes on end, nibbling all surfaces in fine detail. With such attention, any skin parasites are likely to be preened off. She preens the larger chick so intensively that it tries to get away from her.

All macaw couples are different. At this nest, the father always feeds the chicks. In another nest, the father always feeds the female, never the chicks. One male almost never enters the nest. At another nest the male never screams. At yet another nest, the male screams whenever he arrives, and the female comes out to meet him. One female almost never comes out of her nest. Some males deliver food hourly, some about every three hours. A male who takes too long might get a scolding. "I was watching once, and it looked like the female was looking and listening for the male, awaiting his arrival. When the male arrived the female seemed *annoyed*. She was making all grumpy sounds"—Gaby mimics an annoyed macaw, *eh-o-eh-o-eh-o*—"like, 'Where *were* you?'"

Older parents are better parents. Gaby says, "The young breeders, they make mistakes. Parenting improves by repetition." Experience creates competence. One female, Gaby is telling me, "is a super-mom. She could raise anything."

While we continue our vigil under the tarp, each breeze in the treetops rains seeds, flowers, and bugs onto our awning. But the air at ground level does not move. The mosquitoes like it this way.

All the while, other macaws are chattering beyond green veils of forest as, overhead, a hawk turns circles. Gaby explains, "It's not a kind that's a threat to them. So none of them has given an alarm call. But when it's an eagle that's dangerous to them? They all go crazy."

A couple of years ago, researchers arrived at a nest to find the parents screaming just after climbing weasels called tayras had eaten both chicks. "The parents made a sound we've never heard before," Gaby recalled. "It sounded so sad. They spent a few days just mourning like that." Don had told me that one day at the lodge, one of the Chicos was sitting on a railing. On the ground right beneath him was an orphaned chachalaca—a chicken-like bird—that people at the lodge had been feeding. "All of a sudden, we hear this absolutely ear-splitting alarm call. I look up to see a black hawk-eagle coming down straight and fast, probably aimed at the chachalaca but for all practical purposes also flying straight at the macaw." Suddenly, as the Chico on the railing had leaped into the air at the sound of the alarm, his wild mate streaked in and smacked the hawk-eagle. "That was one very unhappy hawk-eagle." Don's take-home: "A macaw will make contact with a dangerous predator that is aiming at their mate. And in this forest, that is about as far as you can go for one you love."

After macaw chicks leave the nest at about three months of age, they sit around in nearby trees for about a week. "The young ones are not strong fliers," Gaby explains. "They don't have full-grown wing and tail feathers. And," Gaby emphasizes, "they are *dumb*. They don't understand the world; they don't know what to do." They are clueless about dangers and predators. "They do a lot of sitting and waiting for the parents."

Gaby points out that "after young fledge, the rainy season is over and the amount of fruit in the forest is declining—a lot." Parents continue feeding chicks for months after they're out and flying. After a week or so, youngsters begin following their parents, learning what's food by watching and sampling what their parents are eating. "They have to learn *how* to be macaws."

⚜ ⚜ ⚜

In Costa Rica, Sam Williams directs the Macaw Recovery Network. (Most of the Central American forests that macaws need have been cut down, mainly for cows, largely so U.S. fast-food burger chains can sell cheap beef.) Williams and his team reintroduce captivity-hatched fledglings to life as free-living birds. Their breeders—mostly scarlet and great green macaws—are rescued captive birds that would not survive release. But for young birds to go free in a complex world without parents to follow and learn from—without their cultural guidance—is a slow, risky gambit.

In all free-living parrots that have been studied, nestlings develop individually unique calls, learned from their parents. Researchers have described this as "an intriguing parallel with human parents naming infants." Indeed, these vocal identities help individuals distinguish neighbors, mates, sexes, and individuals— the same functions that human names serve.

Sam tells me that when he studied amazon parrots, he could hear differences between them saying, essentially, "Let's go," "I'm here, where are you?" and "Hello, darling, I just brought breakfast." Researchers who develop really good ears for parrot vocalization and use technology to study recordings show that parrot noise is more organized and meaningful than it sounds to beginners like me. In a study of budgerigars, for instance, birds who were unfamiliar with each other were placed together. After a few weeks, their calls sounded similar. Black-capped chickadees can distinguish members of their own flock from those of other flocks. So it seems that many birds know who they are and know familiar individuals.

We will see in the next part of this book how sperm whales

learn and announce their group identity. Parrots and even young fruit bats learn the dialects of the crowds they're in. Ravens know who's in, who's out. Too many animals to list know what group, troop, family, or pack they belong with. In Brazil, some dolphins drive fish toward fishermen's nets for a share of the catch. Other dolphins don't. The ones who do sound different from the ones who don't. And orca whale societies have pods, clans, and communities. Each community avoids contact with members of another community. Many animals have a sense of group identity.

Many young birds need to learn important things by observing their parents and elders. Parrots probably need to learn more than most other birds. That's why trying to restore parrot populations by releasing birds born in captivity is risky. It's not as simple as showing young or orphaned birds what counts as food while they're in the safety of a cage, then just opening the door. "In a cage," Sam Williams says, "you can't train them to know where, when, and how to *find* that food. In a cage they can't learn about trees with good nest sites. Just throwing birds out when we haven't prepared them for survival would be unethical." Worse, it might fail. Chances of survival for released individuals is much lower if there are no free-living elder role models. When biologists tried to reintroduce a species called the thick-billed parrot to parts of the southwest United States, where they'd been wiped out, there were no free-living role models. All the released birds died. Conservation workers could not teach the captive-raised parrots to search for and find their traditional wild foods or avoid predators such as hawks. If they'd had parents or a social flock, they would have learned these things as a normal part of growing up.

Elders appear important for social learning of migratory routes, too. Various storks, vultures, eagles, and hawks all depend on following the cues of elders to locate strategic migration flyways or important stopover sites. These could be called their migration cultures. Famously, conservationists have raised young cranes, geese, and swans to follow a microlight aircraft as if it were a parent on first migrations. The young birds culturally absorbed knowledge of routes, then used that knowledge in later seasons on their own self-guided migrations. Four thousand species of birds migrate, so Andrew Whiten of the University of St. Andrews in Scotland speculated that following experienced birds could be "a potentially very significant realm of cultural transmission."

Young mammals, too—moose, bison, deer, antelope, wild sheep, ibex, and many others—learn crucial migration routes and destinations from elder keepers of traditional knowledge. Conservationists have recently reintroduced large mammals in a few areas where they've been wiped out, but because animals released into unfamiliar landscapes don't know where food is, where dangers lurk, or where to go in changing seasons, many translocations have failed. Among fishes, guppies, bluehead wrasse, and French grunts introduced by researchers into a preexisting group follow residents to feeding and resting areas. They continued to use these traditional routes after all the original fish from whom they learned them were gone. We humans inherit ways to dress, and foods to eat, and the music we hear. Often we are not even taught them. From birth, we are simply immersed in our elders' ways, and their ways become our ways. That's how it is for many animals.

When you simply look at free-living birds and other animals, you don't usually *see* culture. Culture makes itself felt when it gets disrupted. Then we see that the road back to reestablishing cultures—the answers to the questions of "how we live in this place"—is difficult, often fatal. In Williams's operation, ex-pets have proven to be the worst candidates for release; they don't interact appropriately with other macaws and they tend to hang around humans.

Williams describes his procedure as "very much a slow release." First, his team trains birds to use a feeder. With that safety net, the birds can explore the forest, gain local knowledge, begin dispersing and using wild foods. Some rescue programs declare success if a released animal survives one year. But, "a year is meaningless," Williams says, "for a bird like a macaw that doesn't mature until it's eight years old."

I ask what they're doing for those eight long years.

"Social learning," Williams' immediately replies. "Working out who's who, how to interact, like kids in school."

To gain access to the future, to mate and to raise young, the birds Williams is releasing must enter into the culture of their kind. But from whom will they learn, if no one is out there? At the very least they must be socially oriented to one another. To assess the social abilities of thirteen scarlet macaws who were scheduled for release, Williams and his crew documented how much time they spent close to another bird, how often they acted aggressive, things like that. When the bird scoring lowest for social skills was released, he flew out the door and was never seen again. The next-to-lowest didn't adapt to the free-living life and had to be retrieved. The third-lowest social scorer remained at liberty but stayed alone a lot. The rest did well.

All of the above sums up to this: A species isn't just one big jar of jellybeans of the same color. It's different smaller jars with differing hues in different places. From region to region, genetics can vary. And cultural traditions can differ. Different populations might use different foods, different tools, different migration routes, different ways of calling and being understood. All populations have their answers to the question of how to live.

Bottom line, said Williams: There is much going on in the social and cultural lives of species such as macaws that the macaws understand—but we don't. We have a lot of questions. The answers must lurk, somewhere, in macaw minds.

"Sometimes a group will be foraging in a tree," Williams adds. "A pair will fly overhead on a straight path. Someone will make a contact call, and the flying birds will loop around and land with the callers. They seem to have their friends."

As land, weather, and climate change, some of these differences will turn out to be the answers of the future. Others will die out. Cultures are sometimes more diverse than gene pools (humans are a great example). Species survival will become more likely if cultural diversity remains. If pressures cause regional populations to blink out, a species' overall odds of persisting dim. With populations blinking out, odds for maintaining the rich and beautiful life on planet Earth become lower.

Williams's goal is to reestablish macaws where they range no longer. It often takes a couple of generations for the descendants of human immigrants to learn how to function effectively in their new culture; it may take two or three generations before an introduced population of macaws succeeds at becoming wild. In other words, macaws are born to be wild. But *becoming* wild requires an education.

For 50 million years, parrots flew where the mood took them. No parrot suffered the indignity of clipped wings, went insane with loneliness, plucked themselves bare, or ached for affection and normal society. No one talked gibberish to parrots or taught them foul language. For 50 million years no parrot heard a chainsaw, or witnessed its nesting tree cut down, or its forest felled and burned and filled with scrawny cattle.

Parrots were made for a world that made them and provided everything. The world knew who parrots were. Parrots knew their world. The world of parrots was among the richest and the most *beautiful* realms of that original world.

BEAUTY

THREE

NIGHT STILL KNOWS HOW TO be night here in the rainforest. The swollen moon reflects ample light, but the forest path is a hazard of roots, so Don and I switch on our headlamps and we tramp through the shadows of great trees to the river's edge. As the trills of pygmy owls fall away, howler monkeys begin revving up their pre-dawn prayers. From deep within their big throats, sounding like some cross between Himalayan throat singers and gravel in a blender, they send through the treetops sustained roars and reassertions of their claims, reconvening the world.

When we step into the wooden boat, the lingering darkness seems to amplify the sound of our footsteps. I watch the Southern Cross through *Cecropia* trees as we get into the swift flow of the Tambopata River and motor a short distance upstream. The sweep of my light makes small fish jump along the black water. It also reveals that the air just above the water is flecked with zigzagging bats.

Beaching the bow on a small island, we step onto the silty

bank and walk to the island's far side. The shifting river abandoned that farther channel about twenty years ago. In its place
has grown a reedy marsh. Across this marsh are bluffs of clay,
eroded and exposed in the rushes and floods of the river's former presence here. Atop the bluff the thick rainforest erects a
sudden vegetative wall. Rising beyond even this, an enormity of
a kapok tree pierces the forest skyline. Sometimes called *Ceiba*,
sometimes considered sacred, this tree overspreads the jungle
below, its umbrella dwarfing even the other rainforest monarchs,
an emperor among royalty, a great and generous presence. Over
the towering kapok tree, one bright planet, Venus, shines above the
Amazon.

A giant kapok tree

We get situated as the night goes to sleep. We're seated, comfortably enough, with our binoculars and a good view across the reedy old river channel to the reddish and beige layers and crumbling folds of the clay bluff. We ready our notebooks and sip some coffee, waiting for day to wake.

As the night's shades rise and the eyelids of morning begin to open, the world retells its creation story. I was expecting something like the explosive dawn chorus of springtime in the Northeast U.S. But here the sun comes up slower. And so does the chorus. It starts with chanting.

Dawn's main soundtrack begins with razor-billed curassows, who call like this: *Whooooohh*, like a turkey-sized dove. The curassows' coos get overlaid by the three soft whistles of an undulated tinamou. These two calls together create one of the most beautiful things I've ever heard. Their slow rhythm feels like the whole forest is breathing.

Don, who has brought me into this new magic, notes the approach of two scarlet macaws. The sun is not up yet, and the birds are just screeching silhouettes in the sky.

While the sky is still blue-gray, others appear on the soundstage. Oropendolas begin calling, their notes sounding like big drops of thick liquid. Motmots begin adding their rhythmic tom-toms. Their notes are so meditative and soothing that they set my mind adrift like a boat in long swells. Rise. Subside. I am afloat on an emerald sea amid shoals of birds. The volume comes up, comes up, until we are wrapped in the songs and calls, some melodic, some emphatic.

It literally dawns on me that countless generations of singers who've continually come and gone have performed this soundtrack of renewed existence daily here for countless thousands of years.

And if all was as it was supposed to be, there'd be no end in sight.

Expanding light brings waves of added chatter. Titi monkeys who sound birdlike, the occasional flute of a white-throated toucan, the whistle of a hawk. And much else. A great antshrike chitters and squeaks and rattles so full of energy that I can't decide whether it seems filled with jubilation, trepidation, agitation, or anticipation. Perhaps he knows no such differences. A kiskadee—white eyebrows and yellow belly—pops up in bamboo. He regards us not at all, disregards us entirely. This is very reassuring.

Don offers that we are in the sweet spot here. First of all, the forest remains intact. Second, in places where wildlife is hunted, it's either already shot out or the survivors hide; you don't see them. Where there are no people at all, wildlife is wary; you don't see much. But where people are a consistent presence *and* don't hunt—like here, near the research center and lodge—animals relax and you get to see them going about their normal lives, doing what they do, being who they are.

As Shakespeare wrote, "I like this place and willingly could waste my time in it." We're near the middle of Peru's Tambopata National Reserve and Bahuaja-Sonene National Park, totaling 5,275 square miles. Immediately beyond these protected areas, forests are cut down and burned by loggers and squatters; water channels are spoiled and polluted with mercury from illegal gold mining. But for now the reserve and its miracles remain safe-boxed. Tourists' money is key to keeping this portion of forest locked from harms.

The question, Don says, "is whether this huge protected area is really big enough to protect the many thousands of parrots that live in it." Is it enough room for viable populations, long term?

I want to know everything there is to know about this place. But not right now. For just a few minutes I want to feel what there is to feel, to inhale this new oxygen, notice each sight, sound, scent; hear each call, distinguish each note in the orchestra, pay attention, and then relax and let the great music wash over me. Only a fraction of such ambitions are possible. Nonetheless I permit myself the luxury, a few moments' indulgence, while there remains the room and the time for it, in this un-ruined corner of the world.

Tambopata River in Peru

The ode to joy that enlivens this planet, our home, generates information, of course. And it generates joy's by-products: mystery and tragedy. The tragedy is that we humans have so overwhelmed ourselves in an "information" age where our own signals crisscross and messages bombard us and everything beeps for our attention—so we've stopped listening. The whole world continues calling out.

For a few minutes, I *am* listening. This tropic dawn, slow-handed as love, rushes nothing. It savors its own time as it celebrates its daily rite of passage.

But I have come for parrots.

Just as the streaky clouds get edged with a palette of pinks, a few amazon parrots arrive on shuddering wings. "Amazon parrot" sounds like one species; there are two dozen. These new arrivals are called "mealy amazons" because their mostly-green backs look lightly dusted with flour. The first mealies land in favored trees at the far end of the bluff across the marsh. The bluff is about a hundred feet high and takes its name, Colorado, from the clay's reddish hue. There above the clay, the parrots talk talk talk.

Some animals are social and often travel in pairs even within larger groups. Humans are such animals. So are macaws. Even in flocks, you can usually see that it's a flock of pairs. A flock of twelve is clearly six pairs of two. When one macaw arrives alone, it's unusual enough for Don to comment, "That scarlet macaw probably has a mate back home in a nest."

I'm having a hard time understanding how Don is differentiating the macaw species, and even the smaller parrots, at such distances in low light. Seeing me struggling to see differences even in the big macaws, Don says, "Scarlet macaws have longer tails that are a bit wiggly in flight." He points to four birds flying below the tree line above the clay bluff. "The red-and-green macaws have stiffer tails, and their heads are proportionately larger."

Okay. Yes, I can see now that the biggest macaws' silhouettes are often quite enough for a positive ID. But all these smaller parrots? To me they all look similar.

The sun is still low, but it is now striking the highest fliers, suddenly making the scarlet macaws coming from high above the forest canopy look like lit embers crossing pale space.

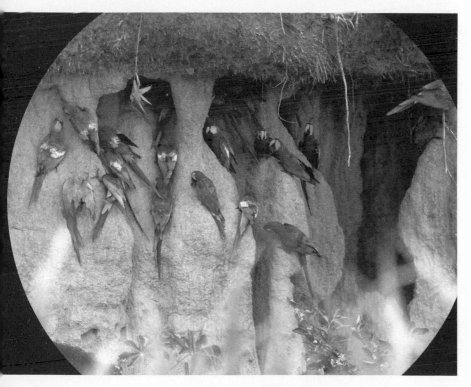

Macaws mining clay

It's a brightening morning with a blueing sky. "Perfect clay-lick weather," Don says cheerfully. *All* the parrots are commuting in for one reason: to eat clay. No other "clay lick" in the Amazon attracts so many kinds of parrots. Seventeen species come here, including six species of macaws: the big red-and-green macaws, scarlet macaws, blue-and-yellow macaws, and three smaller species.

As commuters continue arriving, their sounds build tidally, a slow crescendo. For millions of years the main sound in Earth's atmosphere was the messages birds exchange. Birds remain the most noticeable free-living animals, coloring the world with dazzling palettes of sound. Go almost anywhere. Subtract the motors. Listen.

As more and more parrots come filtering in at an accelerating pace, we are hearing far more than I am seeing. And now I am having a problem. A few minutes ago I was learning the calls of birds new to me: curassows, tinamous, guans, kiskadees, and jays. I hear them all, and they all sound different. Each sings a real song, easy enough to learn and to distinguish from all other callers. But in the various parrots and parakeets—probably a dozen species here already this morning—and in the macaws that I've come here to focus on, I hear only noise getting louder. They seemingly have no repeated call or song as so many other birds do. To me all the parrots simply sound similar, and harsh. To me, they all squawk. I can't make *any* sense of parrot noise.

Don expresses measured sympathy. "It's hard," he acknowledges, adding, "Scarlets have more of a dog-growly voice."

Lifting his pencil from his clipboard, Don points for my benefit. "Hear the red-and-greens?" he says in all earnestness. "They have the most distinctive call of all the macaws here."

If you imagine being a fast-moving parrot in a low-visibility rainforest, you can appreciate the crucial need to hear and recognize individuals, and to be heard as an individual. Experiments with recordings show that females distinguish calls of their own mates and will come out of a dark nest cavity for the sound of the right male. In fact, their individual voice differences can be seen when recorded sounds are turned into graphs, called sonograms. When parrots are being so noisy as they move, a lot of what they're doing is staying in touch and knowing who's where.

But as a beginner here, I can't yet sort through all their sounds.

The smaller parrots, especially the little cobalt-winged, arrive in flocks so cheerfully disorganized that their own scatter identifies them. For people who've seen only caged or wing-clipped birds, it may seem surprising that free-living parrots are *highly* competent fliers. They fly right, left; they land, then switch from one tree to another. A small flock of orange-checked parrots flashes by, sounding full of their own lives.

In this bewildering open-air cathedral, my struggle to see and hear so many distinctions is frustrating. But it is also thrilling. The parrots' excitement in being alive is contagious; it inoculates the very air.

"Dusky-headed parakeet arrival." With each new shot of birds, Don jots their time and numbers. "White-bellied parrot arrival." He tells me white-bellieds nest communally; they travel in stable family groups of six or eight. "Blue-headed *Pionus* parrots arriving straight across." With due diligence Don makes his notes. Without looking up he says, "Another small group of white-bellieds going left, low." Don hears their identity.

If Don's ability to detect the different macaws by voice is

impressive, his ability to pick out the different smaller parrots' calls seems supernatural. *How* is he doing it?

Busy taking notes, he says only, "With captive birds, they're all over the place as far as the sounds they'll make. Wild ones, you can hear the different voices."

Actually, I can't. But the fact that he can means the birds must find it breezily easy to hear all the differences. How much information, and emotion, and intention, might these hot-blooded flocks be sharing?

Parrots, "songbirds" (roughly half of the world's birds, about four thousand species), and hummingbirds can learn their vocalizations and can vary them based on individuality and social learning. The vocal repertoire of other birds such as gulls, hawks, owls, herons, loons, albatrosses, and the rest appear to be more pre-programmed, as human smiling is. The ability to learn new and different vocalizations exists—as far as is known—across an odd smattering of other animals: humans of course, but also bats, elephants, dolphins and whales, seals and sea lions, goats, damselfish and Atlantic cod, perhaps certain insects. With a list like that, there must be others.

The vocalizations often serving dual purposes of territorial claim and competitive advertising for a mate are usually called "songs." "Calls" are for staying in touch, close contact or bonding, identification as when parents and young are searching for each other, and so on.

Songbirds learn their songs and parrots learn calls. In the 1930s, Amelia Laskey plucked a nestling mockingbird from the parents and raised the bird in her home. Honey Child learned to mimic the birds outside her home, the whistle of Laskey's husband summoning their dog, the washing machine, and the mailman calling. Lyrebirds take copying to extremes, mimicking chainsaws and car alarms. Parrots use their sound-copying ability to identify themselves and others.

A human baby cries instinctively, without learning. Many nestling birds utter instinctive food-begging calls. Just as baby humans *learn* to speak the human language they hear—but cannot learn to sing like a lark—a lark listens to the song they hear most: their father's.

As in human children, young birds have a window of time, a couple of months in the birds' case, when learning comes easily. In some parrots and a few others, this window stays open longer and closes more slowly. A young bird will begin babbling snippets of adult notes it is learning by hearing. This is quite like a human baby's babbling. Meanwhile, researchers working with finches have recently revealed that adults "alter the structure of their vocalizations when interacting with juveniles in ways that resemble how humans alter their speech when interacting with infants."

Eventually the song (or songs) and callings that emerge will be the ones that the bird has a mental template for learning and the throat for singing. It's like reading music and playing it on a particular instrument. With practice the bird develops control. Regionally different versions are called "dialects."

More than a hundred studies have been published on dialects in birds; it's definitely a thing. And it's not just birds, but a wide array of animals. As the great conservation biologist Tom Lovejoy commented to me, "Any social animal creates their own dialect, whether it's a flock of parrots or kids at summer camp."

Including some fish. "Cod particularly," said Steve Simpson

of the University of Exeter, "have very elaborate calls compared with many fish." You can easily hear differences in recorded calls of American and European cod.

Yellow-naped amazon parrots in Costa Rica use three regional dialects (North, South, and Nicaraguan). They learn the dialect of the locale where they are raised. When individuals move into other dialect areas, they acquire the local dialect. The talent some parrots show for learning human words reflects their natural ability to learn and distinguish changing parrot dialects during normal life in the wild.

Earning control over sounds requires practice for babies, for musicians, and for birds, too.

Scarlet macaws

The first scarlet macaws that I can see really well material-
ize out of mists rising from the forest canopy in the warming
morning. Arrayed as two pairs, these four land in the tip of one of
the tallest trees atop the bluff, alongside a pair of red-and-green
macaws. And when the first sunrays to drill through the mist
strike them directly, they all seem to simply ignite. Their color is
exquisite.

BEAUTY

FOUR

"LOOK." DON POINTS, "IN THAT cecropia. Three blue-and-yellow macaws just landed. They've got to be a family. Two parents and last year's chick."

My binoculars find them as the early sun sets their gold bellies aglow. Their foreheads look aqua and their blue backs grade to indigo on their shoulders, wings, and tail. They have a striking black throat strap and their white cheeks show elegant black scrawls that differ from individual to individual. The young one is begging for food, with quivering wings. The parents don't react.

"Year-olds have a kind of lost look about them," Don says. "They sort of just look around while the adults are very seriously taking in the scene and evaluating things."

They join a small group of macaws flying along the clay face to land in favored trees that have nice, safe leafy cover close to the clay that is their destination and objective.

The clay contains sodium. Sodium is crucial for animal health and cellular function, and there is almost no sodium elsewhere in this region. So they come here to eat the clay.

What parrots do, they do in groups. You don't see single parrots on the ground. They wait for reinforcements. In the trees their numbers build, noise levels build.

Don says, "You almost get the feeling they're goading each other, trying to encourage someone else to be the first to go down."

Suddenly the amazon parrots—hundreds—begin fluttering to the ground, covering the bare clay with their green bodies like an instant lawn of birds. Despite shoulder-to-shoulder packing and a few jostles, there are no fights. I can see through binoculars that the clay where they are is crumbly. The eating is leisurely. Many stand holding a foot-full of dry clay, nibbling it like a child with a big cookie.

Meanwhile the big macaws remain hesitant. They continue gathering. Most of two hours passes.

When the scarlet macaws number about sixty, their collective chatter escalates in intensity. Don says simply, "The sound builds as they get up the gumption to go down."

What are they on the lookout for? Crested eagles. Ornate hawk-eagles. Black-and-white hawk-eagles. Forest falcons. A harpy eagle. Cats including margays and ocelots, jaguars and pumas.

Don says their vigilance pays. It's nearly impossible for a sharp-clawed hunter to surprise such a sharp-eyed group. "They've developed a very predator-resistant system."

Eventually their group decision to go onto the clay is accomplished by individuals dropping to lower branches, slowly approaching the bare clay slope of the bluff, until a lone blue-and-yellow macaw boldly ventures where no macaw has gone today, onto the clay itself. Once that spell is broken, more land, crowding closely.

This is not wet clay. It must be chipped or chiseled. With much effort of their can-opener bills and thick tongues, the macaws gouge into the hardened slope, prying crumbles.

Some chip a chunk and fly away with what Don calls a "to-go box." They take it to a nearby branch, holding it like an ice-cream cone, nibbling leisurely. Later, in deep forest nests, sodium-rich clay will be in the food fed to their chicks.

They are here for the sodium. But this is also the big social scene. And parrots are *very* social. For them there is more here than just clay and sodium. Parrots *need* to socialize, and as in human cultures, they spend time and energy to go places simply to be with others of their kind. Relationships are being maintained, developed, or begun.

Don points out two white-eyed parrots sitting together, touching each other, but facing outward. They're in a big flock. But as this one pair indicates, within the crowd relationships are forming like stars being born out of cosmic nebulae.

At first, each bird keeps a little individual space around themselves. Then one individual may begin to enter another's personal space. At first they might squabble a bit. But then, proximity inside the personal space is tolerated. Next they move from tolerating to interacting. And then they sit next to each other with feet touching, looking out at an angle like these white-eyed parrots we're watching. At this point they're operating as a pair.

To human eyes the process is "insanely subtle," Don says. It's another way that parrots differ from other birds. Many other birds have more ritualized courtship: specialized dances, synchronized flying, courtship feeding; bowerbirds even build elaborate courtship structures reminiscent of wedding bowers. By contrast, the parrots' free-form proximity is not even as ritualized as a high-school dance.

Like young humans, the macaws indulge in certain fads. Sometimes for months they'll go almost exclusively to one section of the clay face. Suddenly they'll shift to a new spot for a few weeks. And then, maybe they'll go back.

"It's like going to the hot club where everybody's going," Don says. "Then, suddenly, another club is hot. No real reason. No predicting it. There's behavior that doesn't make sense to me."

Actually, one aspect of culture is: It doesn't *have to* make sense. Culture *is* often arbitrary. One human culture wears funny hats; another culture wears different funny hats. Our hats never look funny to us; they're just our hats.

Some animals seem to have evolved an ability to do things *for no particular reason*. Humans have this ability. Parrots seem also to have this ability. Sometimes, when parrots are in a flock and one pair starts preening, many pairs in the flock begin preening. "I think there's a lot of careful watching going on."

Don says he's been in places where flocks of amazon parrots stay quiet. The difference: there, people hunt parrots for the pot; they eat them. The parrots understand that they are saying something that can be heard, overheard, responded to, and even used against them. They *are* all listening. Despite all this noise an entire flock may suddenly go silent. Sometimes only the ones on the clay face will spook and the ones in the trees stay put. Or a particular scream will make them *all* leave the theater for the rest of the day. There seems to be, within all the noise, a great deal of paying attention to one another, not just calling but *listening*.

Joanna Burger studies bird behavior and was my PhD advisor. I knew Joanna's adopted red-lored amazon, Tiko, for many years. Tiko, who would often watch vigilantly through the windows, uttered different, recognizable alarms for "hawk" or "cat." Tiko was hatched into captivity; he lived to be sixty-six years old. It's possible that his fears were innate and his words self-invented. Wild parrots, with their long traditions and rich social interactions, might possibly fine-tune informative vocal and behavioral messages that all nearby parrots can understand.

When Joanna said to Tiko, "I'm going to the garden," or "I'm going to the office," Tiko flew correctly to either the office door or the garden windowsill. This suggests that parrots, with their complex vocabularies, can extract meaning. Or at least they can learn names of places.

A range of beings from parrots to apes to dolphins have, in captive settings, learned to understand and even produce words and phrases that refer to things. Chimpanzees and bonobos can learn to use hundreds of symbols. A border collie named Chaser, dubbed the "world's smartest dog," knew specific names of more than one thousand toys and objects, and could get each one when asked.

African gray parrots can learn to use dozens of human words and phrases to identify and ask for things. A specific training technique is required. There must be two humans who demonstrate, who socially interact, and who take turns using the words to refer to and act on the things—items, shapes, colors—in question. As the parrot begins learning, the humans must adjust the pace of teaching. Without these techniques, the birds usually *don't* learn that certain words mean certain things.

During the learning period, the parrot will often practice in private. After a parrot thoroughly gets it, they will sometimes invent their own labels for things by joining words. Alex, a closely studied African gray parrot, combined words to refer to new things. For Alex, an apple was a "banberry," part banana, part cherry. Alex used the verb "go" to express requests ("Wanna go chair"), announce intent just before acting ("I'm gonna go away"), and demand that a trainer "Go away." This shows that parrot minds need to learn things *socially*.

One pair of scarlets lands at the outer branches of a tall tree. These two start fooling around, hanging upside down, billing and gently biting, their wings flapping like flickering lights in the leafy greenness. When socializing, macaws often hang upside down and goof off. It appears that parrots have a sense of humor, or fun; at the very least they are quite capable of being in a good mood. The flirty birds are probably young, like teenagers. Leg bands applied by researchers have shown that macaws know each other well enough to travel together as a group of young friends.

For macaws, particularly, their entire body is a flag of identity. Tracts of tiny facial feathers create unique patterns of stripes and dashes, like tattoos. Some scarlet macaws wear wide yellow shawls while some carry narrow yellow shoulder scarves. In those fields of yellow, some bear dense blue dotting. Others, sparse.

Many territory-holding birds recognize neighbors. Mockingbirds for instance, don't fuss much with each other after their boundaries are settled, but aggressively drive off any new intruder. Hooded warblers recognize the song of their neighboring territory-holder year to year, even after migrating south, wintering, and migrating back north to their breeding territory. Seabirds such as terns, gulls, penguins, albatrosses, and others recognize their young among hundreds by voice and, in some species, scent. Various primates, crows, dogs, wolves, and horses recognize their group members by voice *and* on sight. (This is likely true of many social mammals.) Pigeons, crows, and jackdaws can recognize familiar individuals of *other* species. Our chickens, and a hand-reared orphan owl, are thoroughly at home with our dogs but flee in panic if a friend arrives with an unfamiliar dog. Birds are extremely sharp observers and know acutely what's going on, who is in their world and in their presence.

A preference by females for males who sing the local dialect has been documented in Galápagos finches and African indigobirds and others; it's probably widespread.

The macaws play and spar, sometimes locking feet with one another and tumbling through the sky. Social knowledge in the mind of each individual travels with them to wherever they might meet. As they get to know each other, sort out dominance, flirt, and bond, relationships made here can be carried with them as easily as a beakful of clay. Anyway, their dangling upside down, their flapping and fooling around, looks like fun. It looks like joy in living.

Some people would say I'm attributing human emotions to non-humans, that I'm guilty of anthropomorphism. I'm not attributing. I'm observing. You can see things in parrots that you don't see in other birds. Parrots play, parrots mimic, parrots prance in rhythm with human music. Finches don't, and gulls don't. This is not anthropomorphism of parrots, nor attribution. It is understanding, based on observation.

Only a few of the roughly ten thousand species of birds seem to play and fool around for the fun of it. The *most* playful of them are crows and parrots. Like playful mammals such as rodents, carnivores, and primates, playful birds chase, play fight, and toss objects. Captive rooks will play tug-of-war with a strip of newspaper while they're standing in many strips of newspaper. Online videos show ravens using a piece of plastic for sledding down snowy roofs and car windows and cockatoos dancing to music. One online video shows a group of swans surfing the crest of a wave into the beach, then flying back out to catch another wave.

Play is practice for skills needed in life, but what *motivates* animals to play isn't their concern that someday they'll need the skills they're practicing. They play because it feels good.

The bright colors of macaws look beautiful to us. But we've mentioned that the reason they have bright colors is that they look beautiful to *macaws*. Birds have bright colors because bright colors attract mates. Birds *appreciate* the colors and females choose the brightest males. Charles Darwin wrote that birds, "have nearly the same taste for the beautiful as we have."

Imagine a world without beauty. Beauty makes life worth the effort, the risks and the frights and the struggles that being alive requires. Beauty is what *eases* that effort into joy. Beauty makes our smiles, and gets us past the tears. I think that is what all beauties have in common, from the sight of a macaw and the song of a thrush to the deliciousness of good food, the touch of a loved one. Beauty makes us love what it takes to live.

A taste for the beautiful exists as a deep capacity, bequeathed to us through inconceivable ages, shared to varying degrees by many creatures. It appears to me that a sense of the beautiful exists to let living beings feel at home, happy, and alive, here on Earth.

And behold these macaws, having such fun dangling around. Aren't they, in their splendor and playfulness, just so surpassingly *beautiful*?

Scarlet macaws

BEAUTY

THE WRAP

MACAWS DON'T *SEEM* TO HAVE much culture. But when things change, we see that they must learn to be wild. Or to exploit people. They are hyper alert. They live a vivid existence. By behavior, and by voice, they communicate many things among themselves. They are smart. They are fiercely loyal to their mates. And when they're young they are especially curious and eager to learn. Parrots raised in captivity don't know how to be free-living, any more than you would know how to be a traditional hunter in the Arctic or the rainforest. Like you, they have to learn. They need teachers. Or, at least, they need to be around experienced elders whose skills they can copy. Not too different from us in that regard. We need to be around people who show us how to do people things that will let us be able to take care of ourselves and others. Parrots need to learn how to be parrots doing parroty things.

Most parrots are green because their small size makes them vulnerable to predators, and being green makes them hard to see among the leaves. Macaws are so big, they don't have many predators to worry about. And they are so careful and vigilant they hardly ever get caught by hawks or ocelots or other rainforest hunters. They really don't need camouflage, so they are very bright and splashy with extravagant coloring. That coloring isn't an accident. They look beautiful to us, sure. But the reason they are so colorful is that they look beautiful to other macaws. Like humans, they have a sense of the beautiful. When looking for mates, they are attracted to bright and colorful individuals. When they choose to mate with the most colorful other birds, their offspring carry their parents' genes for bright, beautiful colors. Think of many kinds of beautiful birds—peacocks, say. And think about the incredibly colored fishes on coral reefs. It turns out that living things often have a taste for beauty, and that through the choices of individuals over countless generations, life itself has created much of the beauty of the living world.

Off the island of Dominica, a sperm whale dives.

REALM THREE: RAISING FAMILIES

SPERM WHALES

Dominica, Caribbean

They say the sea is cold, but the sea contains the hottest blood of all, and the wildest, the most urgent.
—D. H. Lawrence

FAMILIES

ONE

AT 8:00 A.M. WE ARE already traveling over deep ocean. The vast majority of the life on Earth flows through the universe below. And that includes the whales who share our air but make their lives by tunneling through the sea.

How does a whale find meaning in life? It's a very serious question that will take us far from our comfort zone.

Already, I feel our exposure out here. Our thirty-foot boat, an open one, is crowded with gear, crew, four assistants who bring curiosity to their adventures, plus Shane Gero. Plus me. We're running southwest into waves that are getting higher. And the captain, a huge dreadlocked Caribbean man with a boom-box voice named David Fabien, is taking these seas much too hard. I am on the boat's windward side and am soon fully drenched with ocean spray. I know this is his way of testing me, so I don't give him the satisfaction of turning around to glance at him. I've met far worse water and far meaner people. I figure that my taking flying sheets of seawater in stride will ensure that he and I will be good for the duration of this trip.

Meanwhile Shane is shouting, "We couldn't believe it." Another wave showers me. He continues, "That first month, I really got to know sperm whales as individuals. It was spectacular." He's telling me about his first experience here off Dominica in these Caribbean waters.

We soon encounter several dozen deep-flapping, circling, dark-winged birds. Frigatebirds.

And under them, a long, slick patch of water informs us that we have just missed seeing some successful hunting. The hunters' dark, dolphin-like fins are slicing the water. A frigatebird hovers, then plucks a squid from among the large swimming animals.

Shane and crew

I don't recognize whose fins are driving up the squid, but Shane instantly knows them. "False killer whales. *Pseudorca.*" About a dozen and a half of them breathe and roll their round black heads, relaxing now like people after a big breakfast who don't feel like clearing the dishes.

Before we move off, Shane leans over and says, "That soaking was entirely for your benefit."

I tell him, yes, I know.

"He'll take it a little easier from now on."

And we continue. And he does.

We seek a classic sea monster: the sperm whale, the great whale of human imagination, Jonah-slurping Leviathan of the Bible, catastrophic smasher of the ship *Essex*, Ahab-maddening star of the classic book *Moby-Dick*. This is the whale that looms largest in human minds. To this, the world's largest creature with teeth, we now seek the closest possible approach.

For centuries whales have *represented* things. They've represented commerce, jobs. Adventure. Money. Danger. Tradition and pride. They've represented light and food. They are raw material, like iron ore or petroleum, from which many products can be made. And for all these things whales have been targets. Men saw in whales everything—except whales themselves. To see real things always requires honesty.

From this boat we seek the actual creature, living their authentic life. The mammals most specialized for water, whales descended from land mammals who slowly reentered the sea 50 million years ago. Scientists call whales "cetaceans," from the Greek for, basically, sea monster.

But for the next several weeks I hope, with Shane's considerable help, to narrow the gap between us. I seek encounters that will enable me not just to see Leviathan, not just to observe sperm whales, but to penetrate past the labels and feel the whales being themselves, living with their families, sharing the air where our two worlds meet. I seek merely the miraculous, and for that I am positioned in exactly the best of places: a mostly wet, hard sphere in third planetary orbit from a star called Sun, the place where miracles are so cheap that they are routinely discarded. Hard to believe, I know. Let us proceed.

The ancient Caribbean island named Dominica helps form an arc of several volcanic isles that enclose the Caribbean Sea on their west flank and confront the open Atlantic to their east. Dominica's northern neighbor is Guadeloupe and across its southern channel rise the peaks of Martinique. Very deep ocean presses blue shoulders tight against these isles.

Sperm whales inhabit a wider swath of Earth than any other creature except humans, ranging the ocean from 60 degrees north to 60 degrees south latitude. But humans seldom glimpse them. They haunt open-ocean waters of profound depth, almost always distant from land. Here in Dominica, though, very deep water close to land makes this the best place in the known world for a shore-based team to attempt to reach and record them.

Shane has basically said, "We're going to study one of the largest and most elusive creatures in the world when they come and go from this local area." Shane has invested a lot of time and effort in making this audacious proposition work. Failure isn't an option; the stakes are too high, for him—and for the whales.

A curtain of light rain envelops us as we approach our first stop. We are hunting Leviathan, yes—but not by looking. We'd be very unlikely to find them by just riding around and searching for a whale's blow, because sperm whales spend about fifty minutes of every hour underwater, hunting in black and frigid depths thousands of feet beneath the waves. So, we'll listen.

A waterproofed microphone called a hydrophone gets let down over the side. Shane's assistants note location coordinates, conditions of sea and sky. He passes me the headphones; we take turns listening for the clicking of sperm whales' sonar.

I hear water sloshing at the surface. It takes a few moments to get my brain to filter out the water noise, to listen deeper. Then, yes, I hear calls. Squeaks and whistles, very high. Not very loud. Shane says these are probably the false killers we saw way back there under the frigates. Yes, the calls travel far.

The sperm whale sonar we're searching for goes *click, click, click*. That, we are not hearing.

The sea is a swirling mosaic of moving currents and seasonally shifting temperature boundaries. So inhabitants of the open ocean move continually. Tracking optimal temperatures and, mainly, food, they live nomadic lives of epic breadth and depth.

A mere thirty feet down, the pressure has doubled. Sixty feet down the pressure is three times what it is at the surface; the water is so hungry for your heat that if you were skin-diving it would soon chill you, and only a few colors penetrate while the light dims.

Both land and ocean have shaped who whales are. Whales are vertebrates, and they're mammals. Vertebrates evolved in the ocean, mammals evolved on land, and then some returned to the sea, becoming whales. Fish gave to all later vertebrates our basic body plan, including our skeleton, organs, jaws, our nervous, circulatory, digestive, and other systems. When fish brought this blueprint ashore, land and air worked to turn rudimentary limbs into walking legs and flapping wings; turned scales into feathers and fur.

But when some mammals went back to the tides and immersed again, water reminded them about fins. You can sense history in whales' flippers; they're like mittens hiding the same finger bones I'm using to type this sentence. Returning to the sea after millions of years, the reimmersed mammals also hung on to: lungs, their internal heat furnaces, and parental care of their young. They packed their acute intellects and high-minded social skills into their dive bag.

These attributes, developed on land, confer devastating hunting advantages to sea creatures who possess them. Seawater's oxygen content is less than 1 percent and for animals that breathe water with gills, this has consequences for exertion. But air is about 20 percent oxygen.

Quick witted and communicative, sucking densely oxygenated air into their fast-burning musculature, whales and dolphins are hot-brained and über-aerated super-predators from another realm who run rings around their prey.

The sea offered returning mammals two main advantages. One, food swarms. For less-than-large creatures in the sea's open vastness, safety comes *only* in numbers. So small fishes and squids travel in crowds quite unlike anything on land. Often by the millions. Another advantage: water's sound-conducting superiority. Visibility in the ocean is only a hundred yards under the best circumstances. Just a few hundred feet from the surface, no sunlight reaches. But, being about eight hundred times denser than air, water is very friendly to sound.

When hunting, sperm whales produce sonar clicks at about two per second, a rate like: "one and two and—." "Click" is the word scientists use, but depending on distance it can sound like evenly spaced ticking; or, closer, like castanets; or, very close, like steel balls clacking.

Shane consults the GPS for his next position. We go the three kilometers. A sperm whale's sonar can be heard over at least five kilometers. So our listening stops are spaced to leave no sound gaps. If whales are present, we will detect them.

Shane Gero is driven. Trim and athletically built—a lifeguard's physique—with short brown hair and blue-gray eyes, he combines a likeable, undefended friendliness with a deep-ranging, inquiring mind. Shane has made these questions his quest: How does a sperm whale learn who they are? How do sperm whales teach their children to wield the codes of their identity? Getting answers would reveal how sperm whales construct their remarkable sense of family.

The second listening stop was quiet. As we head toward the third, the sea reflects a glaring haze that scatters light everywhere. The distant island, Dominica, fades in and out of blanketing clouds. Moving across the sea surface feels as if we're skating over mysteries. We are.

Our zooming hull scares up flyingfish; one lands in the boat. I admire its large eye, mirror sides, and the indigo streak along its back. Then I flip the fish into the sea.

On our third stop, I hear an engine. But wait. Through the sound of the distant ship—clicks.

Sperm whales click. But Fraser's dolphins, too, can click. And now we see traveling dolphins coming upwind in the glare.

Shane listens intently, headphones on, eyes closed, trying to filter a click out of the sounds of the ocean. To cut some of the noise, he immerses a "directional" microphone. It's just a hydrophone inside a salad bowl on a broomstick, a comedy of high tech meeting highly improvised. The bowl shades the mic from sounds other than those from the direction it's facing. Turning the stick localizes sounds. It's as close as we can come to cupping our ears underwater.

Shane quietly says, "Yes. Could be four, maybe five whales—" He pauses while continuing the turning of the salad bowl. "One's northeast. Most are south of us."

In high anticipation, we look south. It's very rough there. We go a short, wet distance.

Our day is about whales. About finding whales. About identifying who we find. And these vague clicks are how this day begins allowing us to peel its secrets. Far below and far away, sperm whales are hunting, clicking to determine what's ahead in their darkness.

Sperm whales live *vertical* lives. Light and warmth, air and breath, are up. Babies are up. Food is down. During the bright sunshine of our days, the whales spend most of their hours searching inside perpetual darkness. The greatest daily rhythm maker in our human lives—the day-night cycle—doesn't matter much to these whales.

Leviathan inhabits—and creates—a world of sound. Almost constantly they hear the sounds of dolphins, of other whales, and of their own family. Almost constantly while they are deep under-water, they generate and listen to sonar clicks.

The sea shimmers with callings and affirmations. Warnings. Hellos. Yearnings of love-desire. Tribal chants. Engines, ships. At eight hundred times the density of air, water conducts sound four times faster than air, making water a superb medium of com-munication. That's why so many animals from shrimp to whales have developed ways to make the sea transmit their aural mes-sages. Blue and fin whales, booming at the lowest frequencies, can stay in contact and travel "together" while spaced across hundreds of miles. The ocean is brim-full of sound and messaging.

The sonar of sperm whales is the most *powerful* burst of focused sound made by a living thing. That we might hear it across five kilometers in any direction from the whale means that the whale is literally causing the vibration of several cubic miles of seawater, a vast high-power sphere of sound, an extraordinary envelope of energy.

So powerful and penetrating are their sonar clicks that sperm whales can likely see what many things look like inside, as if x-raying them. Humans who get in the water near sperm whales sometimes get scanned with rapid bursts of clicks. When one photographer attempted to push a too-inquisitive baby away from his camera, the baby's head was vibrating so violently from the clicks, wrote James Nestor of BBC News, "that it paralysed the researcher's hand for four hours."

When we stop, Shane submerges the directional hydrophone and immediately announces, "Some to the north."

Our pace accelerates. It feels like a hunt.

After several kilometers, we stop. And this time, clear and

even, I distinctly hear a sound like a fingernail slow-tapping on a hard countertop.

Sperm whales. Definitely. Then the taps stop.

"They might be heading up."

When sperm whales stop hunting they stop making sonar clicks and simply begin a long ascent toward the sun to replenish their breath.

Shane insists that in the time that has passed since the clicks stopped we should be seeing the blows of at least one whale at the surface.

We stare into the glaring chop, searching for evidence of breath. The ocean is pure glitter.

The headphones report faint and distant clicks far to the northeast.

Shane says, "Wow; they're just super spread out today."

But the whales can easily hear each other. For them, being able to hear their family members counts as "together."

"Okay," Shane instructs. "Let's go northeast, try to pick up the main group, see who these are."

Shane was the kind of kid who raised tadpoles in kiddie pools and watched caterpillars become butterflies. By eight he wanted to be a marine biologist. When he was twenty he saw a wild whale. Awestruck by that experience, he wrote an email to *the* pioneering sperm whale researcher, Hal Whitehead. Many weeks of waiting followed. No answer came. Then Whitehead responded, and Shane's life changed.

Before Shane and Whitehead first sailed into these waters,

Dominica was rumored to have "resident" sperm whales. Scientists had never observed "resident" sperm whales. But in the first hour in these waters they met a whale family they named Unit T. Later they met whales they dubbed the Group of Seven—and spent an unprecedented forty-one consecutive days with them. Soon they met half a dozen other whale families.

Now we hear by their sudden silence that the whales who'd been to our northeast are coming up. Pressure, temperature, and light changing drastically, the dissolved gases reexpanding into their collapsed lungs, from a world we do not know they rise up toward the surface of the sea.

Captain Dave announces, "Blow!" And Shane shouts, "Yesss!"

About two hundred yards away, a whooshing left-angled puff of gray steamy breath jets from a massive head. That head is a gigantic ocean-splitting wedge that spans a full third of her entire length. Unlike all other whales, her blowhole is not atop her head but at the tip, where you'd expect nostrils on a typical mammal's snout. A muscular mound controls the opening and clamping shut of the weirdly left-angled single nostril.

The wet vapor dissipates in the breeze. She cycles several more breaths. Breathe. Ten or twelve seconds pass. Breathe. Another twelve seconds or so. Breathe. She is purging her carbon dioxide and recharging her oxygen-freighted blood. Because their lungs collapse from the pressure of deep dives, sperm whales' blood cells pre-pack the oxygen into muscle before the next dive.

She moves toward us. The skin of her head is taut, like dark shrink-wrap. The rest of her body is wrinkly to reduce water drag.

Her eyes, of limited use in black and frigid depths, are relatively small. On a typical day she'll be down for forty to sixty minutes, hunting where sunlight cannot pierce, swim a couple of miles, then rise. Her commute time to the food-bearing depths—often three thousand feet down—is about ten minutes. There she uses all her special gifts and superpowers. Her size makes the hourly depths-to-surface round-trip a realistic proposition. Her sonar overrides the blackness. Her blubber defeats the cold. All her extremes are perfections.

Sometimes they surface in synchrony: *Pfff, pfff, pfff, pfff.* Sometimes they unite at the surface, getting physical, rolling with each other, rubbing, caressing with their short front flippers, running their mouths along each other, producing lots of "codas" and buzzing each other with their sonar. Sometimes they suckle each other's babes. Sometimes when descending in a deep dive, they're together, touching each other. What does it tell us that they love to touch?

She blows and then, dipping that massive muzzle and bending her long back, she hoists aloft her wide black propeller. Weightless in the water but heavy in air, her flukes and sturdy tail-stock shove her downward into the swallowing sea, away from sunlight and air, toward hunting depths perhaps a hundred body lengths down.

"Well," Shane says inconclusively. "Interesting."

I am left with this impression: A whale is too big to see. At a time, you get pieces. Now the head. Now the back. Now the flukes. Never the whale. In Rome once, I said to my wife, Patricia, "We've now seen Michelangelo's painting of the Creator. But what would the Creator's own painting of Creation look like?" I think that is easy to answer now: It is these whales, in this sea.

"She just focused her sonar on us," says Shane, still listening. "Now she's traveling down."

Captain Dave says, "She look like a teenage whale, y'know."

"Yeah, not a big one. But I don't think that's who we were first hearing."

The question remains: Who? Which family?

Suddenly, four hundred yards from us a different whale blows. She's beating a white path through the waves.

Suddenly just a boat-length away, a whale only about fifteen feet long pops up.

Shane yells, "*Neutral! Neutral!* Mom's right here!"

I look down and am astonished to see a huge whale. The mother is resting vertically in the water, nose up. I can't quite see her tail; she's too long.

When sperm whales sleep, they sleep vertically. "They kind-of bob up to breathe." Whales always have to breathe intentionally; it's never automatic.

The small whale is making short shallow dives. She's nursing.

Milk is the mother in liquid form; the growing infant mammal is entirely its mother's milk transformed into flesh and blood, bone and all the growing organs and systems, the pulsing and purring. Most sperm whales nurse for four or five years before weaning.

In a family Shane calls the Group of Seven, a youngster named Digit was about five, and had stopped nursing, when, about a year ago, she got tangled in some fishing gear that slowed her down. After Digit's movement was compromised, her mother, Fingers, began nursing her again. Digit is still dragging the gear around— and is still being nursed.

*   *   *

For sperm whales, family is everything. In Shane's early years here, the Group of Seven liked to hang with a family called the Utensils. An adolescent female of the Utensils named Can-Opener liked to play with the Group of Seven's young ones of that time, named Tweak and Enigma. Interestingly—"hauntingly" might be a better word—since Digit's tangling the two families have continuously remained together as if they are one. Is it because they recognize that Digit is in distress? (The rope tangling the base of Digit's tail will likely cut into her as she grows, and probably kill her. But Digit is still moving too fast for a human rescue attempt.)

Families such as these who particularly like one another are called "bond groups." It's a term borrowed from elephant researchers, and it designates families who are good friends. In fact, the social structure of sperm whales more closely resembles that of elephants than of other whales. Elephants and sperm whales both have tight, stable families of females and dependent young. Females of both remain in their birth family for life and give birth into the same family in which they were born. Male elephants leave their mother around adolescence. Sperm whales, the same.

A typical hour of a sperm whale's adult life consists of a long dive—traveling down to food, searching for food—between surface breathing intervals of ten minutes or so. But sometimes they rest and socialize at the surface for a few hours.

The young one goes into a dive. Young whales don't usually do that, but—

"Codas!" shouts Shane.

Short bursts of clicks are coming through the headphones.

"Codas" are not the steady ticking of whale sonar. Codas come as varied rhythmic patterns, a little like simple Morse code. They are sperm whales' signals of identity. By signaling with their codas, they announce themselves, determine the identity of other whales and whether they've encountered a group that they can socialize with or must avoid. The whales often make codas during transitions such as when going to the surface or about to dive, when greeting family members, when a male is present, if they've detected predators, or when a baby is born.

Through the headphones come codas *so* loud, I think at first that it is Captain Dave clapping his hands behind my head, messing with me. I'm amazed at the clarity and strength of their talking. They're going: One. Two. Three-four-five.

No one fully understands what information is coded into those patterns. Except of course—all the whales do.

The mom who'd been sleeping is now exchanging codas with another whale. There is a back-and-forth, a call-and-response: "I am here," one says. "And I am over here," says the other. A conversation of sorts. Perhaps the youngster had dived because she went to greet whomever is approaching.

And now, yes, another adult female appears with Mom. The three whales rest at the surface side by side, breathing. Youngest on the right, the largest on the left. One senses deep relaxation after deep exertion. Each forceful, intentional exhalation wafts faint rainbows into the breeze.

The larger two whales slide below for a bit of rest. After she's been sleeping for just a few minutes, the small whale begins tail-slamming the surface. The youngster seems to want action. We count twenty-one slaps.

"He's like, 'C'mon, Mom, wake up,'" Shane laughs.

Meanwhile, Shane has been listening to two other whales, who sound like they are a couple of kilometers away. They fall silent.

Moments later, yet another whale explodes full body out of the ocean about three hundred yards away. And as she crashes back she seems intentionally to slam her head on the sea surface for maximum effect. On a second vault she bursts into the air with jaw open wide, water streaming from the corners of her mouth. Through four more breaches, her strength and mass astound us.

Her name is Jocasta. The edges of the whales' tails are remarkably irregular. They bear scratches, gouges, and bites, perhaps from sharks or false killer whales. Such lesions and lacerations heal but don't grow back into shape. The set of woundings life inflicts on each whale are unique enough to allow positive IDs. Jocasta has two scallop-shaped marks. These whales are hers, the J Family.

Jocasta the sperm whale

FAMILIES

TWO

LONG AGO, SPERM WHALES—WORLDWIDE—DEVELOPED
the capacity to understand group identities, distinguishing families and groups of families called "clans." The way sperm whales recognize and announce identities and group membership is with their codas. Sperm whale babies go through a babbling period similar to human infants' (as do young monkeys, apes, dolphins, and some birds). By the time they're a couple of years old, they've learned the family's codes. As young children learn the language of the group they are born into, young whales learn the codas of their family and clan. The whales are always individuals within families, carrying on their lives in detail that is as vivid and present to them as ours is to us. Across the open ocean and in deep darkness, "what they have," Shane has come to appreciate, "is each other."

About two dozen families of sperm whales come and go from these waters. Of these, Shane knows ten families intimately enough to recognize them on sight by the shapes of their tails. Others, Shane has seen only once in his fifteen seasons here.

Sperm whale tails differ

Shane explains, "The main thing I've learned from whales is that who you're with makes you who you are. If you're a sperm whale, your family is the most important thing."

For centuries the only thing humans cared to understand about whales was how to kill them. Almost too late, we acquired a little respect. Now, with the help of people like Shane, we are starting to understand whales a little.

Shane seems deeply affected by humanity's relationship with whales. He adds, "We need to find ways to coexist. These are rich, complicated lives. No one notices. And that is painful, because *I know them.* And I struggle with how to make people care. I've had fifteen years so far to try to figure out what it means to be a whale. They've helped me be a better human being. Now I have to figure out, What am I gonna do—*for them?* That keeps me awake."

❧ ❧ ❧

When we think of culture, we first think of *our* culture. We think of computers, airplanes, fashions, teams, and pop stars. For most of human cultural history, none of those things existed. For hundreds of thousands of years no human culture had a tool with moving parts. Yet human hunter-gatherers held extensive knowledge, knew deep secrets of their lands and creatures. And they experienced rich and rewarding lives.

The value of cultural diversity in the human family has been underappreciated and many cultures have been lost. The importance of culture in the other-than-human world has been almost entirely missed. We are only just beginning to recognize that even in many other species, what is learned and shared is often crucial to survival.

A baby sperm whale has a lot to learn. Deep-diving skill develops over time. Young learn diving gradually by accompanying their mother and other adults. Before they can use their own sonar, they likely "eavesdrop" on information in the returning echoes of the sonar of adult family members, learning the sounds of detection, and of pursuit. The answers to other questions must also be learned. Where in these currents and underwater slopes is the hunting best? How do we travel? Where do we go in changing seasons?

When a devastating drought hit East Africa in 2009, hundreds of elephants died. Of fifty-eight elephant families in Kenya's Amboseli region, one family lost twenty members while the "KA" family did not lose anybody. The KAs were led by two big females—Kerry and Keira—who were forty and thirty-nine years old when the drought hit, old enough to remember where water remained during other severe droughts. "Old enough for wisdom," as the legendary researcher Cynthia Moss described them to me. "They are obviously doing something right and I would attribute that to the knowledge of those two old females." Without receiving knowledge from older keepers of knowledge, they'd die. That is culture.

Before the 1960s, many people thought dolphins were little different from fish. Starting in the 1960s, Ken Norris showed scientifically that a key to being a dolphin is flexible learning. Flexible learning leads to different behaviors from group to group. By the end of the 1980s, Norris and others were viewing the group differences in dolphin behavior as "clearly cultural."

Local habits or particular traditions can keep individuals together—and *also* keep groups apart. Community markers that enforce difference can even keep groups on hostile terms. Humans sometimes carry this to extremes (think of languages, flags, uniforms, and so on).

Group identity and self-identification with a group are not exclusively human. The Pacific Northwest's so-called "northern resident" and "southern resident" orca communities' only apparent difference is how they sound—their "dialect." Yet the orca communities avoid mixing, for purely *cultural* reasons. Researchers said this has "no parallel outside humans." But, it turns out, cultural identity and cultural segregation are more widespread. The whales seem to prefer a group they're familiar with, where everybody does things the way they're used to doing them.

Certain bats, birds, and many others recognize individuals by the sounds of their clicks, howls, trumpets, and songs—their voices. Because voice *represents* the individual, voices are *symbols* of identity. Alarm calls are likewise *symbols* for a dangerous predator. Apes, monkeys, and birds have alarms for things like snake, hawk, and cat. They are essentially words for these different dangers, telling companions whether to look up, look down, or climb a tree.

❦ ❦ ❦

Sperm whales live in stable groups because they need reliable babysitters. Infant sperm whales cannot accompany their mothers down into the great, black, frigid, high-pressure depths where adults hunt. Babies often trundle along at the surface in the direction of sonar clicks coming from foraging adults far below, or turn circles while awaiting the ascent of their elders. Waiting at the surface, they are quite defenseless. Killer whales (orcas) are rare, but they are real and pose mortal danger for baby whales.

The solution has been for baby sperm whales to live with aunts and their grandmother, all in constant contact using sound. Any distress signal brings the whole family right up.

"When killer whales show up, it seems like sperm whales suddenly come popping up out of nowhere," Shane says.

Other large whales solve the problem of newborns quite differently. Most large whales give birth in tropical locations, where mother whales continually stand guard. The catch: There is no food there, and mothers do not eat for several months. Shrimp-like krill and the vast swarms of small fishes that other big whales eat live in cold climes. So each year mothers migrate to give birth, then migrate to where their food lives. Humpback, gray, and blue whales (the world's largest animal—ever), and others migrate thousands of miles annually.

Sperm whales do it differently. They give birth where their food is. Sperm whales' main prey, squid, live in warmer latitudes. The hitch for them? The squid are two thousand feet down, and infant sperm whales cannot follow. This dilemma, more than anything, drives the sperm whale's social arrangement of living in female-led families where everyone knows one another and everyone protects the young.

Their strong family bonding was first documented by Thomas Beale in his 1839 book, *A Natural History of the Sperm Whale*. Beale got to know these whales from the deck of a whale-hunting ship. He wrote, "The females are very remarkable for attachment to their young." He added, "They are also not less remarkable for their strong feeling of sociality or attachment to one another."

※ ※ ※

The largest creature with teeth, sperm whales can clamp onto squids that are the length of a living room, squid species bearing names such as "giant" and "colossal." Battles ensue. But *most* squid that they eat, such as the diamondback squid here off Dominica, are around three feet long. And many are much smaller.

What they *don't* eat is people. Previous authors wrote nonsensically of sperm whales seeking human flesh. Beale described them—correctly—as, "remarkably timid, and . . . readily alarmed . . . endeavouring to escape from the slightest thing which bears an unusual appearance."

And so here Shane and I are in these waters, seeking murderous monsters of legend who are in reality timid and bonded to family, who treat their children, Beale wrote, "with the most unceasing care and fondness."

❦ ❦ ❦

A cultural group is a collection of individuals who have learned, from one another, certain ways of doing things. In a culture, Shane is saying, "you are who you are because you're with who you're with. Because of who you're with, you do what you do in the way that you do it."

The cultural differences among sperm whale clans include different clans' distinct movement and diving patterns, hunting strategies, and so on. But before different groups can establish their own different ways of doing things, individuals must be able to identify themselves *and* must determine whether others belong to their group—or not.

A sperm whale clan can have many families and anywhere from dozens to thousands of whales. They self-identify by their dialect of clicked codas. All members of a clan may socialize. If they don't share a dialect they will avoid contact and socializing. Sperm whale clans constitute a kind of national or tribal identity. Only in sperm whales and humans do group identities involve so many individuals.

Shane explains, "Each whale must learn their social traditions. Behavior is what you do. Culture is how you've learned to do it. Culture gives clans their sense of identity and their ways of doing things." Raised in a different place among different individuals, you'd be part of a different culture.

Shane emphasizes, "They live by the difference between 'us' and 'them.'" In many ways, so do we. Dogs, too. When my wife and I are on the beach with our dogs Chula and Jude running loose, they meet other dogs and say hi to other friendly people. Often they'll engage in some play with other doggies or indulge some petting. But if we simply keep walking they stick together, wait for each other, then come and join us. They never want to go off with other dogs or other people. Our dogs know the difference even between new and familiar dogs. On the beach—this is just an example—Chula will stop to check out a new little white dog, then come running over to me as I've continued walking. After our walk we turn around and go back up the beach from where we've come. From a hundred yards away we see that the little white dog is still there. Chula shows no interest. She knows she has already met this dog. But the moment a tan boxer appears on the beach just a few paces from the little white dog, Chula bee-lines to the boxer. She knows this is a new dog whom she wants to check out. Recently we adopted a seven-month-old Aussie shepherd pup named Cady. On Day Two we brought Cady plus Chula and Jude to a dog-friendly beach. We decided to unleash all three dogs. Not only did Cady stay nearby and come when called, but in numerous mingles with other people's dogs she immediately resumed traveling with us. After just one day with us, Cady's sense of belonging was set.

Whales share our air but play, socialize, and live entirely in the sea. All of that makes whales *what* they are. Culture in the form of differing group behaviors and vocal identities makes whales *who* they are.

Humans have human culture. Dogs have dog culture. Whales have whale culture. And who is touching whom under the ocean surface, and whether they are gazing eye to eye, they alone know.

FAMILIES

THREE

THIS MORNING THROUGH THE HEADPHONES I hear—faintly—a humpback whale singing in the far distance. The song contains themes that the whales repeat in specific order. A male humpback will usually complete the song, then repeat it numerous times, singing for hours on end.

The male humpback whale's strange and haunting singing is a changeable cultural aspect of that species. Each year, all adult male humpbacks within each ocean sing the same song. But in each ocean the song is different from the song being sung in other oceans. There's a Pacific song, an Atlantic song, and so on. And each year the song of each ocean changes. The new songs spread wave-like, a slow-moving fad crossing blue infinities from whale to whale, with all the whales adopting the same changed elements of the song. Somehow together, strangely, the whales create a new song. Researcher Ellen Garland and colleagues called this "cultural change at a vast scale."

Roger Payne wrote of the first time he heard a humpback

whale singing: "Normally you don't hear the size of the ocean . . . but I heard it that night . . . That's what whales do; they give the ocean its voice, and the voice they give is ethereal and unearthly." Payne later told me, "The reaction of some people to hearing whales sing is to burst into tears; I've seen that a lot."

The whales continue calling us, asking, in effect, "Can you hear me now?"

❧ ❧ ❧

Our boat is undulating across the massage of long swells. We transit in and out of the company of flyingfish. Of terns. The sea, glittering, rolls like a carpet of short blue flames. We travel in small ecstatic sparks of time.

Out of the chop, from up ahead, comes a large group of dolphins. Short snouts, small dorsals, pastel-pinkish bellies and throats. Medium-sized; a bit longer than a person. I've never seen these.

Shane knows them: Fraser's dolphins, a species unknown to humans until the 1970s. About eighty dolphins, with many small babies. They rise together, and dive together, coming into view through the surface as a bunch and going out of view through the surface as a bunch, so that the visual effect from our side of the sea is as if a group of dolphins is riding a Ferris wheel as they travel. There is such grace in all the exuberant leaping, gravity defying somersaults, sun-sparkled aerial spins, and fun-enriched lives.

The hydrophone goes in just so we can listen to the dolphins' squeals and whistles.

Animals generate signals coded in sounds, scents, songs, dances, rituals, and language. The world is awash in layers and waves of communication.

❦ ❦ ❦

The farther from the ever-more-distant green slopes we traveled, the bluer the sea. The whales inhabit a world without borders. The dark water floating us is fully three miles thick.

We are headed home from this mammal-filled day when a large group of dolphins and their numerous babies swarms us. They are yet another species—pantropical spotted dolphins, known in the biz as "pantrops." They want to ride the wave created by the bow of our moving boat, and they don't ask permission. This is what freedom looks like. I watch them in the clear water. They stream along, pumping and pacing. They leap and plunge and turn sideways to look up at us looking down. Their bodies are dotted individually, some with many spots, some with very few. They precisely exhale streaks of silvering bubbles before snatching a sudden gasp of breath, pursing their blowhole shut, and surging under, all at full speed inside of a second. The water here is sprinkled with a drifting yellow weed and some of the dolphins playfully snatch pieces of it on a flipper as they stream along. Effortlessly. Miraculously.

FAMILIES

FOUR

FOR A LONG TIME A silly debate raged about whether animals (including humans) live entirely by instinct *or* by learning. The debate was called "nature vs. nurture." Genetically fixed instincts such as hunting, communicating, and caring for babies were "nature." Learning and culture represented "nurture." In reality, *both* nature and nurture are involved. Humans can sing, but not like a humpback. Whales cannot learn French. Genes determine what *can* be learned. Culture determines what *is* learned.

A kitten instinctively chases, but kittens who get to watch their mothers hunting become better hunters more quickly than kittens who have to figure out on their own what their claws and teeth and curiosity are for.

Social learning is special. Social learning gives you information stored in the brains of other individuals. You're *born* with genes from just two parents; you can *learn* what whole generations have figured out. Social learning can spread changes in group customs much faster than can genetic evolution, which requires the slow spread of changing genes over many generations.

Let's pause here to clarify that genetic evolution happens slowly in tiny steps. The evolution of whales from land mammals didn't happen because a litter of land-grazers was born with flippers instead of legs. That wouldn't work. Rather the first step was for a wetland-dwelling population to develop the advantage of webbing between their toes like a Labrador retriever. Any advantage of a certain slight difference translates to a few more surviving offspring than the average. That increases the frequencies of the advantageous genes in a population. Many generations later the population might possess the further advantage of having webbed feet like an otter, leading to flipper feet like a sea lion, then to flippers like a seal's that remain like flexible hands in mittens with nails that can scratch an itch, and eventually to the stiff fin-flippers of a whale. Even a whale's pectoral fins still have all the same bones as your shoulder, arm, and fingers. But this takes *millions* of years.

With *culture*, you get skills tailored to what you happen to need, where you happen to be. A dolphin or elephant, parrot or chimpanzee or lion, can tap into skills and wisdom that various members of the group developed and passed along. For a young whale: Where in miles and miles and miles of ocean should I look for food? For a young elephant: Where is drinking water when everything I know has dried up? For a young chimpanzee: Now that all the fruit is gone, what do I eat? For a young elk: As everything begins freezing solid, where will we go for the winter? For a young wolf: How might we hunt and eat this creature that weighs ten times what I weigh? These are all skills learned from experienced elders.

Many things that you crucially need to know, you would never learn on your own. We learn from others who already know. From one another we become who we are.

One definition of culture that is pretty good is: "the way we do things." Behavior is what we do; how we do it is culture. Reach for the leash or your car keys and your dog immediately gets excited that you'll be taking a walk together. That's shared culture. Culture is information and behavior that *flows socially* and can be learned, retained, and shared.

But to have culture, someone must do something that is *not* the way we do things. We can live in an automobile culture because an innovator invented an automobile. We can listen to rock music because one person electrified the age-old guitar. Ironically, culture—a process of learning and conformity about "the way we do things"—depends on someone, at some point, doing what no one has *ever* done. Culture depends on crowds of conformists *and* the rare innovator. Without some original innovator—some untaught learner, some unschooled teacher— there is *no* knowledge, skill, or tradition that could get shared; no culture to copy and conform to.

So even though a baby whale follows their mother to one of the species' traditional foraging spots, the only way such a tradition can start is that, every now and then, someone has to break with tradition and go a new way.

In 1980, one of the humpback whales off New England started whacking the water surface with his fluke several times. This helped scare little fish into tight schools, making them easier for the whale to engulf with his cavernous open mouth. Over several years, one young whale after another copied the technique until most of the population did it.

Humpback whales sometimes swim in a big slow circle blowing rising "bubble nets" around schools of small fishes. It scares the fishes into the center. The whales then come rapidly up through the middle of their big bubble rings with their mouths open. In Alaska, groups with more than a dozen whales bubble-net for fast-moving herring while off New England, where the prey fish are usually the slower-moving sand lance, the bubble-netting parties are smaller. Alaska groups tend to be more stable, sticking together. New Englanders seem more opportunistic. In Antarctica, where whales are just recovering from devastating lows in population numbers after a century of intensive hunting, they appear to be reinventing bubble-netting in small groups of two or three.

※ ※ ※

Each time a sperm whale comes up through the ocean toward the blanketing air, they announce their individual identity and their group membership. Using their codas and their dialects, they show and declare, "This is who I am. This is with whom I belong."

When a family of whales is "chatting," as Shane says, each whale makes a coda about every five seconds. As humans can have language differences, sperm whale clan boundaries are reflected by differences in group codas. The various codas used by a group are called its "dialect."

Often a clan's most commonly used coda is in fact the one that identifies their clan. The second most common identifies an individual, like saying your name is Bonnie. But to identify your family you have to say you're Bonnie Thompson. That's why the third most common coda identifies the family.

The larger of the two clans here makes a five-click coda that has never been heard from any other sperm whales in the world. It goes, one, two, cha-cha-chá. It says, "I'm from the Eastern Caribbean Clan. Are you?"

The other clan's identifying coda goes: one, two, three, four, (beat), one. Shane calls it "4+1." So when whales here are making codas, you'll hear *either* 1+1+3 codas *or* 4+1. These codas could be centuries old. Whales who make the same clan coda spend time together.

The second most commonly spoken coda is five clicks spaced regularly and performed rapidly. Shane says, "That lets us hear two whales and say, 'That's Fingers, and that other one is Pinchy.' Pinchy might make the first click slightly longer and Fingers might make the last click slightly shorter, for instance." Small things, but they're recognizable, like hearing someone say, "Hi," and recognizing their voice.

"In the Group of Seven, Mom tends to start the vocal exchanges, tends to decide to dive first, and she's the most social." The whales can always hear one another calling. That's closeness.

Within families all the whales know one another as individuals, as we know family members in our own homes. Their recognition is as complete and immediate as ours, or as dogs greeting their own people. There's no mistaking.

The third most common coda—the one used to identify the family—is always four clicks. But one family makes a certain *pattern* of four clicks; another family makes another four-click pattern. "We usually hear it only when there are *other* families around," explains Shane.

So—translated into English—the whales can say, "I belong to the Eastern Caribbean Clan. I am Pinchy of family F."

"That is self-recognition and self-identity. That is a community of families and individuals. These whales," Shane declares, "are cultural beings."

FAMILIES

FIVE

THE SPERM WHALE IS THE whale of literature and of bathtub toys. So its strange head is oddly familiar. Ask a child to draw a whale, and you'll usually recognize that head. It can weigh as much as ten tons, and comprise a third of the whale's body length—in larger males it can span *twenty feet* from nostril to eye.

We know now that the high prow of the sperm whale's head is really the living world's greatest sonic boom box. Almost the entire head of the sperm whale is a factory of vibration and amplification. Dolphins use sonar, too, but the sperm whale's head is super-sized.

Unlike our skull, which is rounded at the forehead, toothed-whale fore-skulls are dished into a bony sound reflector. The biggest part of a sperm whale's ocean-splitting wedge of a head, extending far forward of the skull, contains no bones *at all*.

To generate their sonar, they force air across structures called "phonic lips" in the air passage inside the blowhole. A sperm whale's blowhole is, weirdly, their left nostril. (Other whales' blowholes are atop their heads.) Their *right* nasal passage does not exit the whale's head at all. Its sole function is to push air through the "phonic lips." This creates vibration. That's the beginning of how a click is generated. Now the vibration enters a fatty organ that uses lipids of different densities as sound lenses. The energy reflects off an air sac immediately in front of the great bony dish-like front of the whale's skull. The sound then passes through a series of acoustic lenses in the lower half of the whale's vast bulb of a head, which is a gigantic sound-amplifying system. This series of reflections and focusings of the vibrational energy amplifies and sharpens the click. What is emitted through the skin at the forefront of the whale's head is a weapon of sound.

The vibrations emitted from the whale echo back from potential prey and other objects. Returning echoes are first received by the whale's lower jaw (not their ears). Whales' specialized, fat-filled lower jawbones set up minute vibrations that get channeled to their inner ears.

The brain *creates* "sounds" as an *interpretation* of nerve impulses. It's like how a speaker or video monitor creates music and images from digital or analog impulses.

The miracle occurs when the brain displays its analysis and we *experience* the conscious sensations of seeing the world. The sperm whale's head houses the world's largest known brain—about twenty pounds. (Fellow humans, ours weighs three.) No one understands how neuronal processes in our brains result in *felt experience*, our actual sensations.

Might whales (and dolphins and bats)—use sonar to actually *see*? Think of it this way: we see *echoes* of light. Why not see echoes of sound? Commercial sonar sets available in any boat-supply store bounce vibrations off objects, detect the returning echoes, and send those impulses through wires to a display screen where the returning "sound" is made into colored pictures. Might sonar-using whales, dolphins, and bats process the echoes into visual perception? What we know for certain is, they are astonishingly good at knowing where and what things are, at very fine resolution, and at very high speed.

A sperm whale spends about 80 percent of their lifetime propelling that detection device through frigid blackness thousands of feet below our common source of breath. At every moment of our own lives and loves, sperm whales by the thousands are clicking their queries into unbounded spaces of the deep world, traveling with their families.

❦ ❦ ❦

Male and female sperm whales differ mightily in lifestyle *and* size. Females reach about 35 to 40 feet (11 meters or so) in length, and about 15 metric tons. Males are much larger at around 65 feet in length (20 meters) and perhaps 45 metric tons. Females stay in the family of their birth for their entire lives, like elephants do. Males live with mothers for about ten years. Also as with elephants, male sperm whale separation from birth families happens gradually, taking as much as half a dozen years to finally swim into the deep indigo for good.

Researcher Hal Whitehead recorded his first impressions of adult male-female interactions, writing, "The male was the focus of intense attention from all group members. They just seemed delighted that he was there. For his part the male was all calm serenity and gentleness."

FAMILIES

SIX

"Far above all other hunted whales, his is an unwritten life."
—Herman Melville, *Moby-Dick*

SOPHOCLES ARRIVES BACK IN OUR world with a sudden explosive leap and terrific crash, like a school bus bursting from the ocean. This new afternoon promises to be a good one.

A few minutes later *PHOOOSH!*; Jocasta pops up close to us.

Now Laius is up, too, a quarter mile from Jocasta. To them this is no distance at all, and after about ten minutes they all fluke up and dive.

An hour later, Jocasta and Laius surface together two and a quarter miles from where they dived. Add the distance down and the distance up: They've swum about three and a half miles.

All afternoon, the young female named Jonah had seemed alone. But Jonah has been tracking her mother, Sophocles, from the surface, and reuniting with her for part of every hour. Their greetings remind me of enthusiastic elephant family members trumpeting and twining their trunks with family and friends. Or African lions waking from a long rest and rubbing up against each other like the huge cats they are. Or the face-licking, tail-waving "rally" of a wolf pack. Or just the way our dogs greet us in the morning. They don't simply show that they "identify" each other. They demonstrate that they are excited to be together.

And so here's the thing: In the ocean vastness, maintaining family cohesion requires constant effort. It is *intentional.* They are well aware. For being a sperm whale there's no instruction manual, no rulebook. Mostly what there is is the wide deep ocean and family bonds.

Two and a half hours after leaving Jocasta's family, we've traveled southwest about nine kilometers, or five nautical miles. Shane is hearing more sperm whales. He thinks they're a different family.

Most days when there are whales here off the west shore of Dominica, it's only one family unit at a time. Shane *has* seen as many as six families here at once, about thirty whales. That time, a male had arrived. It must have been a good day for all.

But whomever Shane's hearing at the moment, they're faint. And deep. So we move in the direction from which the sound seems a little stronger.

This whale-size cat-and-mouse appeals to me. It's interesting. It's a science technique. It's a hunt. It's a game.

On the next stop the clicks are clear. Whales are near. Suddenly they stop. From under his hat and sunglasses and earphones, Shane says, "Corners, everyone."

And so we station ourselves around the boat, eyes outward.

And in under a minute, "*Blow!*" Just fifty yards off the bow.

When this whale flukes up, Shane instantly exclaims, "Mrs. Right!" The R family also includes Rita, Rap, Ribs, Ruckus, Rim, Riot, and Roger—who is female.

Two other whales that we'd been hearing come up half a mile apart and begin puffing their white clouds of breath. They are Sally of the S's and Roger of the R family, two families known to like each other. Members of the same clan, of course.

Here off Dominica, too, one of the two clans tends to swim closer to shore. A young sperm whale learns the ways of the family from their mother and the other adults. They learn what to say, where to live, how to move, how to hunt. To the question of "How do we live in this place?" each group passes down its particular answers. In a word, they've *specialized*.

Different groups of orca whales are real specialists. One wants one species of salmon. Another specializes in hunting sharks. In the Antarctic one type mainly hunts minke whales. Another specializes in penguins. Another group hunts seals. Other killer whales catch herring. These hidden cultural differences have sent killer whale cultural groups on differing evolutionary trajectories worldwide.

Dolphin communities also often contain hidden structure. Many different dolphin groups specialize in one technique or another, clearly learning from and sharing with their children and friends. Some use one specialized individual "driver" to herd fish toward the others, or to raise a ring-shaped cloud of mud around schools of small fishes. In the Adriatic Sea, two groups of dolphins "time share" the same area, using it at different times. One of those groups follows fishing trawlers for their discarded catches; the other never does. Off Brisbane, Australia, the arrival of shrimp trawlers caused a cultural split: one hundred and fifty-four bottlenose dolphins began following for discarded fish; eighty-eight other dolphins in the same area did not. The two groups began avoiding each other, two new social classes. When the boats depleted their prey and abandoned the area, the pan-handling dolphins went back to hunting *and* they all went back to mixing and socializing.

Sticking to one's group can offer efficiency advantages simply because everyone knows what to expect and how to cooperate. If you're a killer whale hunting fish you want to be in a big noisy group that will scare fish into schooling up tightly, but a group hunting sea lions must deploy in small, stealthy, silent packs. The two strategies are not compatible, so the specialists don't mix.

Knowing who you are, and who is who. Knowing *the way* "we" do things. Thus equipped, sperm whales take their clan member-ship through the worldwide seas.

FAMILIES

SEVEN

SPERM WHALES DON'T BOTHER ONE another, other sea creatures, or people. People nowadays have learned that they can swim with them with no worry other than whether they'll get good photos.

For centuries, most meetings between sperm whales and humans did not end well for the whales. Whale hunters were first to notice that sperm whales had some secret way to call for help.

> *"All sperm whales . . . have some method of communicating by signals to each other, by which they become apprised of the approach of danger, and this they do, although the distance may be very considerable between them, sometimes amounting to four, five, or even seven miles. The mode by which this is effected, remains a curious secret."*
>
> —Thomas Beale, 1839

One day, more than a century and a half later, whale experts Bob Pitman, Lisa Ballance, Sarah Mesnick, and Susan Chivers were watching two groups of sperm whales when they spotted five killer whales heading toward the second group. The sperm whales of the second group then submerged, leaving a baby at the surface for less than a minute before they resurfaced. The scientists wrote:

> We think they may have sounded an alarm call at this time because immediately afterward the first sperm whale group bunched up and started traveling rapidly toward the second group . . . At least four other groups of sperm whales in the distance were charging toward the core group at full speed, pushing waves with their heads.

The scientists noted that, "every sperm whale within at least a 7-km [4.3 mile] radius immediately charged toward the threatened group at high speed and joined them in a defensive formation." Soon *fifty* sperm whales were present. "There can be little doubt but that they were responding to a very specific and powerful acoustic signal."

Then, "they formed a staggered chorus-line formation with the entire group lined up, facing the same direction, side-by-side, apparently touching each other," a "remarkably precise formation."

The killer whales—orcas—decided to leave.

Herman Melville, who had signed on to a whale-hunting voyage in the early 1800s long before he wrote the classic *Moby-Dick*, saw that the more whales were hunted, the more they joined into large groups. He wrote, "Sperm Whales, instead of almost invariably sailing in small detached companies, as in former times, are now frequently met with in extensive herds . . . for mutual assistance and protection . . . You may now sometimes sail for weeks and months together, without being greeted by a single spout; and then be suddenly saluted by what sometimes seems thousands on thousands."

EIGHT

WHAT HAD STARTED AS ROWING men throwing harpoons in a quest for lamp oil and candles morphed into floating factories. Petroleum-fueled ships hunting with cannon-fired explosives had the speed and killing ability to pursue the swifter whales that men pulling on oars could never catch. Blue whales had been inaccessible under sail. Engine-propelled ships killed more than 90 percent of them. For all whales everywhere, the twentieth century tallied approximately 3 million killed. They were used for: dog and cat food, chicken and pig feed, mink food at fur farms, fertilizer, motor oil additive, something called creatine for flavoring manufactured soups, and margarine. Nothing was wasted—except the whales themselves.

Whales help keep the ocean alive. So to kill them is to accelerate killing the ocean itself. To leave whales alone is to help ensure that the ocean will produce more of the fishes and squids that people like to eat. Sperm whales dive so deeply that they bring back what had been long lost to surface waters. Often they poop immediately before diving, delivering to the surface their deeply acquired iron and other nutrients, returning them into sunlit waters where they can nourish and grow the drifting cells of plankton that require nutrients *and* sunlight *and* that soak up carbon dioxide to create the green pastures of the sea, forming the very first rung of the entire ocean food ladder. All the flyingfish we've been seeing, all the fish that chase them, all the birds that eat them, are receiving into their bodies some of the molecular matter raised from the deep eternal darkness by the superpowers of Leviathan.

Leviathan, cachalot, sperm whale: These are just labels. In truth there can be no name large enough to fit this creature— with the largest head housing the largest brain, interrogating the world with the loudest inquiries—living their out-of-sight existence distant from all shores and far beyond words, carrying on life in the fond company of family and comrades. That was true long before any first human had spoken a word, and it remains true to this minute.

We may yet lose them in an ocean of plastics, chemicals, fishing tangles, spinning propellers, speeding hulls, and noise. All whales now have trouble competing with the aquatic primate for the fishes of the seas. The more humans fill the world, the more we empty it.

Yet, we still have whales.

Getting hunted to near extinction may have erased much whale culture. The stakes remain high for whales. It is a distressing story that can be hard to hear, but there is another reason we must not look away: Things have gotten much better.

FAMILIES

NINE

FOR SIX DAYS WE HAVE seen no whales. Today we will try again. I tell Shane that, unlike the last few days, he should stop listening to whale-free water. I tell him, "Just find whales on the first drop."

We get to the first listening spot and lower the hydrophone and—

He's listening. He points. Over to the southwest.

He hands me the headphones. Loud and clear, three or four whales are clicking through the black depth. Wow, I say, nice. Why didn't we just do that for the last six days?

So we go southwest about a mile. Shane listens again and says, "It's gone quiet there." They must be coming up.

We scrutinize the wrinkled sea for a white puff in the million-mirror glare, looking, looking.

Shane's technical assistant, Fabién Vivier, who is French, says softly, "Zere's a blow."

Shane listens to whales

He says a kilometer. Almost two-thirds of a mile. But none of us—

"How sure are you that you saw a blow?" Shane inquires.

"Hundred percent."

We head that way.

No whale.

But when we stop to listen again, the headphones reveal whales in several directions. Shane hears two ahead of us. Three or four inshore. He adds, mysteriously, "Too many whales for my dreams."

Then—"There!"

Definitely a sperm whale blow.

"Okay," Shane requests of Dave, "let's poco-poco ahead."

And as we do, Dave also announces a second "Blow!" as another whale pops up nearby.

But when she flukes up, Shane says, "Who is *that*?"

Fabién calls a third "Blow!" He says it's very distant. This time no one doubts him.

After being underwater for the better part of an hour, a whale's first breath is always sudden and forceful. But this one is so far from us—more than a mile—that I can barely see the drifting vapor.

The two closer-up-ahead whales are now at the surface about a quarter mile from each other.

"Let's go poco-poco toward the closer one."

Through the silvered sea, we slowly motor. The morning sun skips stones of light across the waters, turning wavelets into a million points of bright. Up from this shimmer, into the low haze, come occasional angular puffs of whales breathing. We're doing science wrapped in a tropical dream.

The closer whale ghosts.

We go poco-poco toward the other. For a couple more minutes, the whale continues breathing off used gas, packing new oxygen into the freight holds of her blood.

She flexes and her back rises. She flows forward, nods downward and her flukes rise high, pouring water into the sea. A distinct half-moon is missing from the edge of one fluke.

Shane says, "That last whale, the left fluke seems super familiar."

So—who? We seem to be hearing eight whales here. Shane is trying to determine their identity from the flukes we've just photographed.

"Well," chirps Fabién, "three whales in ten minutes. Good day so far!"

Shane squints into the chop. "It could be the P-Unit. We need to hear their codas."

A small two-family clan consisting of just the P and K families uses an identifying coda having four regularly spaced, even clicks, and then a beat and a click. "Click click click click—click." They don't make the "one plus one plus three"—click, click, cha-cha-chá—coda of the larger clan to which all the *other* families here belong.

We move a short distance. The hydrophone goes down. The headphones go on.

Now they're all down foraging, beaming their pulsed sonar inquiries "one and two and one and—" throughout the enveloping ocean.

"Oooh—buzzing. She's just chased something!" Shane turns the pole and points, saying, "Most of them are over that way."

We go.

Shane had said that most of the whales were over in this direction. Now that we're here, we don't hear a thing. But an hour has passed since they went down, so they're probably traveling upward.

"Okay, let's look for blows."

Minutes pass.

Then, Captain Dave announces, "There! She blows!"

Her size impresses even Shane. "Imagine the changes a whale her size has seen," he says.

Then, blood recharged with oxygen, she hunches and flukes up—and is gone.

"I know this whale," he insists. He thinks for a moment, running a whale-tail catalog though his mind. "I'm just not sure yet."

Meanwhile, the hydrophone indicates three whales far, far down. With his arms Shane indicates their positions, spanning a 45-degree spread. I'm trying to picture what is going on thousands of feet below and perhaps a mile distant. Once, in a close encounter with bottlenose dolphins in the Bahamas, I got a glimpse in miniature of life for a whale with sonar. With mask and snorkel, researcher Denise Herzing and I had slipped into clear water thirty feet deep as four bottlenose dolphins foraged for fish that were completely buried in the sand. Waving their heads back and forth just above the sediment, the dolphins seemed to sweep the seafloor with sound. I could easily hear their sonar buzzing. A couple of times a minute a dolphin would suddenly plunge their snout into the sand to pin and scarf down a thoroughly hidden fish whose hiding hadn't saved it. I was watching the x-ray-like power of their sonic search engine, the most elite hunting weapon in the sea. As they moved leisurely along reaping so hidden a harvest, I watched astonished by their superpower.

Two whales rise together up ahead and raise their breathy flags. They are resting side by side.

Shane says, "To be beside each other means something pretty amazing." In all their years of swimming, staying together in the vast ocean requires effort and persistence; it requires *wanting* to stay together. All their lives they are held by the stickiness of their emotional bonds. That is very special.

These two fluke up and slide downward, and begin making codas.

Shane says, "One plus one plus three." So, these whales are

of the larger clan. But that eliminates only the two families that make up the smaller clan. This could be any of the dozen and a half families of the larger clan.

"Who *are* these whales?" Shane demands. It's driving him nuts.

Listening for whales

❧ ❧ ❧

By looking at the photos we've taken, Shane has ascertained that we've spent our morning shadowing the L Family. Mystery resolved.

An hour later, mysteries compounded, Shane thinks he hears *another family* to the north.

And so the ocean—which can seem so bleak and empty and hostile—seems very alive.

Just a few minutes later a whale rises and blows and breathes.

We poco-poco closer.

It's actually two. A mother and a youngster of perhaps five or six years. They are touching-close, and breathing in sync.

Shane's got the headphones on, monitoring their communiqués. "Mom's talking to her baby."

I wonder what the whales said to one another when they were being harpooned throughout every ocean. On the planet of whales who are talking to their babies, can we make a better deal for ourselves and every other living being in the world? Whales' cultures answer the question, "How best can we live here?" We need to ask ourselves that question.

Mom dives, going deep. I put on the headphones and am amazed at how *loud* her coda-clacks are. These are the codes of recognition, of bonding and belonging. Their sound is percussive and precise, like castanets. Then the codas stop. Mom goes into foraging mode and her echolocation clicks begin coming into my ears. *Tick. Tick. Tick . . .*

The sea rolls below, rolls under, rolls past, massaging us in its rise and subsidence, whispering its rumors. By its sheer physicality the sea itself seems alive. The slowly throbbing swells bear the rippling breath of the midday breeze. Layers of existence, everywhere.

The sea erupts as the young whale we'd seen an hour ago with Mom suddenly leaps clear in two quick massive sideways flops that detonate white geysers. An upside-down third fling delivers a cratering crash. When another whale surfaces a quarter mile away, the juvenile swims over to join her. The juvenile and Mom snuggle, touching-close.

After this little while of sharing the sea air with us, they hunch into their dives. Mom lifts her flukes with high-flying grace. The youngster just humps down, another shallow dive as if trying to imitate Mom but—maybe someday.

We leave these and go northward three miles. We hear whales here, too! Sometimes you go day after day after day without hearing a click. Some days you hear clicks everywhere you go.

"It's whale *soup* out here today!" Shane exclaims.

Half a mile away, two whales surface close together. Half a mile northeast of *them* a third whale is up. "This makes ten adults and a juvenile so far today," Shane reports.

The blue-gray sea is slick and hazy-bright. It is both eternal and instantaneous, and the whales that this ocean has brought forth seem, in their pacing and their scale, to reflect the enormity of all things past and present. Something like time must be passing, but I feel suspended in an infinite moment that seems to vibrate in place. Perhaps from the whales I have learned something about living.

For a little while, I am where I am best, among living creations of greater powers that long preceded me and may long outlast us all. For the duration of the encounter, the beauty and truth of them overwhelms the heartache of what humans have done, cleanses *everything*. For a short interval of time, they have tapped me awake and I feel at home in the world.

Shane is telling me about a whale named Can-Opener.

"Can-Opener made the hydrophone into a game. She'd be waiting, and when we'd lower the hydrophone, Can-Opener would try gently to mouth it, making the crew play hide-the-hydrophone. And she'd come up and circle us, giving everyone on the boat a good looking-over." Shane adds, "When a whale is playing with you, looking you in the eye, you can't resist returning the gaze.

"The whales consider themselves different individuals," Shane adds. "So we have to treat them that way. These individuals are distinct and important to one another." Each sperm whale is *somebody* to other individuals. One implication: The death of such a creature matters to those individuals who survive them. Relationships create an added layer to life. That adds a layer to the meaning of death. Collectively they hold the sperm whales' traditional knowledge about how to succeed here. "If you lose the book about how to survive in the Caribbean, if you wipe that out—"

Shane is worried about his whales. Culture can be innovated and can spread. Culture also can be lost. So what's at stake is not just numbers. What's at stake is: ways of being in the world. What's at stake is communities of individuals who know who they are in the world because they know one another. Think of tribes. Tribes of other beings. Other beings with other minds living other lives on the same planet. Different, certainly. But fundamentally, not really very different. They mean something to one another, and so their lives mean something to them.

That should mean something to us.

FAMILIES

TEN

WITH TIME NOW FOR A break, most of our crew takes the opportunity to jump into the water. "Put your head under, you can hear the whales." Vibrating an enormous sphere of water around them, they sound-saturate the ocean as they level off perhaps a thousand yards down.

Half an hour into their present deep foray, they've clearly doubled back. We drift along in the company of the large juvenile who is waiting.

As soon as a whale pops up in the distance and begins purging her lungs, the juvenile we've been hanging with ditches us.

"Joining Mom" is Shane's safe guess. Another family member slits the sea surface and greets the baby.

I slowly realize I'm no longer seeing "sperm whales." I'm seeing a family.

Shane Gero looks across the ocean. "It's always exciting to see whales," he says, sounding as though there's something he's not saying. "But I really wanted these to be Fingers and Digit and the Group of Seven. But it's not them.

"It's a weird year," Shane says to me. "Weird weather. Many of the whales we are seeing are whales we haven't seen in a long time. We hadn't seen Unit L in almost a decade. We saw them twice this week. Unit T, not for seven years. I want to ask them, 'What have you been *doing* for all these years?' In that time they might have been just nearby, or way across the Atlantic, off Africa.

"This is shaping up to be the first year we haven't seen the Group of Seven. No Pinchy. No Fingers. That was the family we'd spent the most time with, and they became the best-studied sperm whales in the world." He falls silent for a few moments. "Every year when we come here, the most exciting thing is getting to see the whales we'd left. To see the R Family again, and to see how Rap and Riot and Rita have all done in the year we've been away.

"When I named these whales, I had assumed Thumb and Enigma would be here as long as I kept coming." He glances at me.

I ask which young whales whose births he was here for have died.

"Oh," he sighs. "When we met the Group of Seven, Fingers had her young one Thumb. Thumb disappeared. Then Enigma was born. I really liked Enigma. She and her cousin, Tweak, would come to our boat while everyone else was down foraging. And then Enigma wasn't there. I took her death poorly. Then Tweak died. And breeding females were passing away. Puzzle Piece, Quasimodo, Mysterio—gone. The Group of *Seven* dwindled to three." In the last three years, four of Shane's familiar whales have gotten tangled in fishing gear; two have died. Digit is now pulling around stuff she got tangled in. If Digit dies that'll be four babies in a row, in a small family. "That's devastating."

One of every three newborns isn't living to their first birthday. "When young whales die," Shane reminds me, "who will learn their grandmothers' wisdom?"

"They face the realities," Shane says, "of living right next to people." There's pollution, pesticides, cruise ships, cargo shipping, and high-speed ferries. There are plastics to swallow, fishing gear to get tangled in. "We're making their days harder. Lose a family's knowledge of how to succeed as a sperm whale in the Caribbean and you've made a hole in the canvas. Lose enough families in a clan, you lose the whole picture. You lose the ability of a species to succeed." Shane brightens, and adds, "But we've got a new youngster, Aurora, who has lived. So it's not all bad."

This has been the hottest day yet under the punishing dazzle of the disk in the sky. We've depleted all the water we brought. If we need more we'll have to open the emergency box. But the whales have been so generous with their time, it's well worth the heat.

"I owe it to them," Shane explains, "to be a voice on their behalf. To share their stories. To stand up for their existence. These whales are too important for me to fail. So we'll just make it work."

The problems are real, and yet there is life. And some time left. And the many people who care. And because of a few who insisted, there are still whales and a few wild horizons. Perhaps it will always depend on a few who insist.

At 5:00 P.M., two whales burst the surface a mile south of where they dived. We've followed whales all day. Now it's time for us to quit this dream and keep our promises ashore. It's getting late for humans who have miles to go and equipment and boats and data to deal with. And dinner to make and the dishes to wash before doing it all again tomorrow.

❧ ❧ ❧

Nearly a year and a half later, I often recall the privilege of peeking into Shane's world—and the whales'. And then out of the blue, I get this email from Shane:

"I thought you'd be happy to know that Jonah is still with us and getting bigger, Digit has gotten free of her rope and will get the chance to grow old and eventually lead her family. It seems like the high rate of mortality has slowed."

Yes; I am *happy* to know that.

FAMILIES

THE WRAP

SPERM WHALES LIVE IN FAMILY groups. So do elephants, wolves, human beings, and a bunch of other animals. By traveling with sperm whales we've realized that culture gives a sense of identity. It might seem a bit odd that being an individual is not all about you. You get your identity from the social group you're in. You are *who* you are because you know *who* you're with. What have you learned from those around you? You've learned the answer to a pretty important question: How do *we* live? For sperm whales the answer is, "This is my family, this is our group. We do things a certain way. We socialize with certain others. Our ways are different from how other families and other groups do things." Does that sound familiar? It should, because as cultural beings, we humans also form families and social groups in which individuals get their sense of identity from who we are with, and we also live in groups that do things differently from other groups. And our different groups also have different answers to the question of "How do we live?" But the thing that's most important for humans to remember—and maybe sperm whales and elephants know this at some level, too—is that other ways of living are equally valid, and that our ways are as strange as anybody's. They just seem "normal" because they happen to be our ways. Our culture.

Sperm whales together

EPILOGUE

A CHIMPANZEE LEARNS HOW TO pay to play; a macaw casts a covetous eye on a beautiful neighbor; a sperm whale learns who she will be living with. The whole world speaks, sings, shares the codes. Culture creates vast stores of unprogrammed, unplanned knowledge. Culture is the learning that many minds share.

On the ground, this is merely very interesting. But when you zoom out to the biggest picture you begin to realize that our living world, Life on Earth, is a tiny fragment of the universe. Culture is Life adjusting and responding over ages and in real time to the corner of the universe it finds itself in. The magic and mystery of culture is apparent in everything from a singing sparrow, to a million fish following elders on an ancient oceanic migratory route, to the view we get from the latest interplanetary telescope. Life is a small part of the universe that is capable of directing certain aspects of its own destiny. And Life has, in the very realest ways, chosen random acts of beauty, and chosen to see existence as beautiful. Not all life, not all the time, but over time, over the hundreds of millions of years of this wondrous journey, that has been a trend. To understand that Life *has created* a perceptual capacity that is felt as *beauty*, and then has sought more and more of what is beautiful; that Life prefers what is lovely and sees *as lovely* what it prefers, sees beauty in those around it in its bit of the world, in our corner of the sky, in the existence that envelops us all—that is a realization so stunning it quite takes our breath away.

And that makes the miracle of our living world sacred. But sacred doesn't mean safe.

Many skills of living must be learned from elders who learned from *their* elders. If that chain breaks, life gets rougher, everything takes more time, survival drops, and the living world shrivels just a little bit more. Recovery, never assured, becomes more uncertain.

Beings who've succeeded on Earth for millions of years don't seek, and should not require, our approval. They are of the world and they belong as well and as much as any of us. In their groups, in their lands and waters in the original world, they know who they are. Their lives are vivid. They do everything they can to stay alive and to keep their babies alive. That's what most matters in our own lives, too; they are in many ways not so different. We are all of this world, together.

"Who are we with?" That's perhaps the most important question. I've tried to peek with you into the vast answer. A newer question looms: Will we let their kinds continue to exist or will we finalize their annihilation? That's our stark choice.

The living beauty of the world is caused *by* the living things around us. Our ability to sense things as beautiful is the universe's true miracle. Beauty is a constant fact of life, there whenever we care to notice. Can humans adjust our own nature and elevate compassion in time to keep the world beautifully and abundantly alive? Can we evolve a culture for the future of life on Earth? Only humans can ask that question. Only humans need to. And the whole living world depends on our answer.

Life can feel difficult at times. But we can realize how amazing it is that we are alive in a living world. It's much happier to just open the door, step out, and be refreshed. Awe and beauty gift wrap our existence, waiting to welcome us home.

ACKNOWLEDGMENTS

PRAISE BE TO: SHANE GERO and all his compatriots of the Dominica Sperm Whale Project. Praise to the exceptional Cat Hobaiter and the generous welcome I received at the Budongo Conservation Field Station in Uganda and especially Geoffrey Muhanguzi, Kizza Vincent, Robert Eguma, Monday Gideon, and Pawel Fedurek. Praise be to Donald J. Brightsmith, Gaby Vigo-Trauco, Ines Duran, Varun Swamy, Kurt Holle, Gabriela Orihuela, Rainforest Expeditions, and the staff at Refugio Amazonas and Tambopata Research Center, who were just unreasonably generous. Sam Williams of the Macaw Recovery Network helped me make the most out of a chance meeting and a too-brief follow-up. Likewise my perspective was tweaked by Ben Kilham, Phoebe Kilham, Debbie Kilham, and the amazing black bear neighbors of their forests; also too brief, yet mind-altering.

For crucial support I am indebted to Susan O'Connor, Roy O'Connor, the Prop Foundation, Anne E's team, the Gilchrist family and Wallace Research Foundation, Stony Brook University and its School of Marine and Atmospheric Sciences, the Andrew Sabin Family Foundation, the Kendeda Fund, Ann Hunter-Welborn and family, and Julie Packard.

My indefatigable agent Jennifer Weltz is always there, keeping various projects on the rails. Emily Feinberg and Emilia Sowersby made this edition happen.

I thank my wife, Patricia Paladines, for all her many graces. I thank our doggies for keeping the smile in our hearts and their wet tongues on our cheeks. They remind us daily what it looks like to love being alive. We try our best to learn by their example. There is joy and great beauty in all of it.

SELECTED BIBLIOGRAPHY

Beale, Thomas. 1839. *The Natural History of the Sperm Whale . . . To Which Is Added, A Sketch of a South-Sea Whaling Voyage*. Holland Press. Online at Archive.org.

Boesch, C. 2009. *The Real Chimpanzee*. Cambridge: Cambridge University Press.

Burger, J. 2001. *The Parrot Who Owns Me*. New York: Villard.

de Waal, F. B. M. 2019. *Mama's Last Hug*. New York: W. W. Norton.

Ellis, R. 2011. *The Great Sperm Whale*. Lawrence: University Press of Kansas.

Godfrey-Smith, P. 2016. *Other Minds*. New York: Farrar, Straus and Giroux.

Herzing, Denise L. 2011. *Dolphin Diaries*. New York: St. Martin's.

Mann, J., R. C. Connor, P. L. Tyack, and H. Whitehead. 2000. *Cetacean Societies*. Chicago: University of Chicago Press.

McGrew, W. 2004. *The Cultured Chimpanzee*. Cambridge: Cambridge University Press.

Melville, H. 1851. Reprint, 2003. *Moby-Dick*. Dover Thrift Editions.

Reynolds, V. 2005. *The Chimpanzees of the Budongo Forest*. Oxford: Oxford University Press.

Rothenberg, D. 2010. *Thousand Mile Song*. New York: Basic Books.

Stanford, C. 2018. *The New Chimpanzee*. Cambridge, MA: Harvard University Press.

Whitehead, H. 1990. *Voyage to the Whales*. White River Junction, VT: Chelsea Green.

Whitehead, H. 2003. *Sperm Whales: Social Evolution in the Ocean*. Chicago: University of Chicago Press.

Whitehead, H., and L. Rendell. 2015. *The Cultural Lives of Whales and Dolphins*. Chicago: University of Chicago Press.

INDEX

Photographs are indicated by *italic* page numbers.